WANDERLUST WREN

Explore Thailand: A Comprehensive Travel Guide for First-Timers

Stress-Free Tips, Hidden Gems, and Budget Travel Hacks for Effortless Planning

Copyright © 2024 by Wanderlust Wren

All rights reserved. No part of this publication may be reproduced, stored or transmitted in any form or by any means, electronic, mechanical, photocopying, recording, scanning, or otherwise without written permission from the publisher. It is illegal to copy this book, post it to a website, or distribute it by any other means without permission.

Wanderlust Wren has no responsibility for the persistence or accuracy of URLs for external or third-party Internet Websites referred to in this publication and does not guarantee that any content on such Websites is, or will remain, accurate or appropriate.

Designations used by companies to distinguish their products are often claimed as trademarks. All brand names and product names used in this book and on its cover are trade names, service marks, trademarks and registered trademarks of their respective owners. The publishers and the book are not associated with any product or vendor mentioned in this book. None of the companies referenced within the book have endorsed the book.

First edition

This book was professionally typeset on Reedsy. Find out more at reedsy.com

Contents

INTRODUCTION	xi
CHAPTER 1: UNDERSTANDING THAILAND	1
An Overview of Thailand's Geography and Climate	1
The Geographical Layout of Thailand	1
Climate Variations Across the Regions	2
Key Geographical Features and Natural Landmarks	3
Maps and Visual Aids	4
CHAPTER 2: A BRIEF HISTORY OF THAILAND	9
Ancient History and the Formation of Early Thai Kingdoms	9
The Significance of the Chakri Dynasty	10
Major Historical Events and Their Impact	11
Cultural and Historical Landmarks	13
CHAPTER 3: UNDERSTANDING THAI CULTURE AND TRADITIONS	15
Critical Aspects of Thai Culture	15
Traditional Thai Customs and Practices	18
Cultural Norms and Etiquette for Travelers	20
The Diversity Within Thai Culture	21
CHAPTER 4: PLANNING YOUR TRIP	23
When to Visit Thailand: Best Times and Seasons	23

Pros and Cons of Visiting During Each Season	24
Key Events and Festivals Throughout the Year	26
Recommendations Based on Traveler Preferences	29
Essential Travel Documents and Preparations	29
Essential Resources for Travelers to Thailand	31
Embassy Information	32
Visa Requirements and Information	33
Creating Your Ideal Itinerary	35
Budget Travel Strategies	36
CHAPTER 5: NAVIGATING THAILAND	39
Mastering Bangkok's Public Transportation	39
Detailed Guide to Using the BTS Sky Train and MRT Subway	41
Navigating the Bus System in Bangkok	42
Navigating Intercity Travel: Trains, Buses, and Flights	44
Renting Scooters and Bikes Safely	45
CHAPTER 6: AUTHENTIC LOCAL EXPERIENCES	48
Experiencing Thai Festivals and Events	48
Major Thai Festivals	48
History and Traditions Behind Each Festival	53
Tips for Participating Respectfully	55
Engaging with Local Customs	57
Regional Variations and Lesser-Known Festivals	57
Exploring Local Markets and Street Food	63
The Concept of Local Markets in Thailand	63
Must-Visit Markets for Unique Experiences	65
Popular Street Food Dishes and Where to Find Them	67

Tips for Exploring Markets and Street Food Safely	71
Village Home-stays and Community Tours	73
The Benefits of Village Home-stays and Community Tours	73
Recommended Village Home-stays and Community Tours	75
Typical Activities and Experiences Offered	77
Tips for Choosing and Preparing for a Home-stay	79
CHAPTER 7: HIDDEN GEMS AND OFF-THE-BEATEN-PATH LOCATIONS	82
Discovering Northern Thailand's Hidden Treasures	82
Highlighting Unique Natural Attractions	84
Recommending Cultural and Historical Sites	86
Detailing Adventure Activities in the Region	88
Secret Beaches and Islands in Southern Thailand	90
Discovering Lesser-Known Islands	90
Recommending Secluded Beaches	93
Detailing Unique Marine Activities	94
Providing Tips for Sustainable Travel	97
Offbeat Adventures in Eastern Thailand	99
Exploring Lesser-Known Provinces	99
Highlighting Unique Natural Attractions	101
Recommending Cultural and Historical Sites	102
Detailing Adventure Activities in the Region	104
CHAPTER 8: CULTURAL ETIQUETTE AND RESPECT	107

The Dos and Don'ts of Thai Etiquette	107
The Importance of the 'Wai' Greeting	108
Proper Behavior in Public Places	109
Showing Respect to the Monarchy	110
General Social Etiquette Rules	111
Visiting Temples and Sacred Sites	113
Dress Code for Temple Visits	113
Proper Conduct Within Temple Grounds	114
Interacting with Monks	116
Significant Temples to Visit	117
Engaging Respectfully with Locals	121
The Importance of Learning Basic Thai Phrases	122
Navigating Social Interactions	123
The Significance of Personal Space and Body Language	124
Participating in Local Customs and Traditions	125
CHAPTER 9: SAFETY TIPS FOR SOLO TRAVELERS	128
Staying Safe in Urban Areas	128
Situational Awareness:	129
Using Public Transport Safely	129
Safe Accommodation Practices	130
Safety Tips for Exploring Nightlife	131
Avoiding Common Scams and Tourist Traps	133
Identifying Common Scams Targeting Tourists	133
Tips for Recognizing and Avoiding Scams	136
How to Handle Scam Situations	137
Common Tourist Traps to Avoid	138
Health and Wellness Tips for Solo Travelers	139
Staying Hydrated and Eating Safely	140
Managing Travel-Related Stress and Fatigue	141
The Significance of Travel Insurance	142

Accessing Healthcare Services in Thailand	144
CHAPTER 10: OUTDOOR ADVENTURES	146
Jungle Trekking and Wildlife Safaris	146
Popular Trekking Routes and Destinations	148
Wildlife Safaris and What to Expect	150
Tips for Safe and Responsible Trekking and Safaris	152
Diving and Snorkeling Hot-spots	154
The Underwater World of Thailand	154
Popular Diving Destinations	156
Snorkeling Spots and What to Expect	158
Tips for Safe and Enjoyable Diving and Snorkeling	160
Rock Climbing and Waterfall Exploration	162
Rock Climbing in Thailand	163
Popular Rock Climbing Destinations	164
Waterfall Exploration in Thailand	166
Tips for Safe and Enjoyable Rock Climbing and Waterfall Exploration	168
CHAPTER 11: ROMANTIC GETAWAYS	171
Romantic Getaways	171
Secluded Beaches for Couples	171
Romantic Activities for Couples at Secluded Beaches	174
Tips for Accessing These Hidden Gems	175
Nearby Accommodations	177
Luxurious Resorts and Spas	178
Luxurious Amenities and Services	181
Spa Treatments and Wellness Experiences	182
Tips for Booking and Making the Most of Luxury Stays	183
Unique Romantic Activities	185

Unique and Memorable Activities for Couples	185
Romantic Dining Experiences	188
Cultural Experiences for Couples	191
Tips for Planning and Personalizing Romantic Activities	193
CHAPTER 12: FAMILY-FRIENDLY ACTIVITIES	195
Family-Friendly Activities	195
Child-Friendly Attractions in Bangkok	195
Outdoor Parks and Playgrounds	197
Entertainment Complexes and Themed Attractions	200
Family-Friendly Dining in Bangkok	202
Family Adventures in Chiang Mai	204
Nature and Wildlife Experiences	205
Cultural and Creative Workshops	209
Outdoor Adventure Activities	212
Family-Friendly Accommodations in Chiang Mai	214
Beach Activities for Kids in Phuket	216
Water-Based Activities for Children	217
Family-Friendly Beach Resorts	219
Nearby Attractions and Excursions	222
Tips for Beach Safety and Comfort	226
CHAPTER 13: ECO-TOURISM & SUSTAINABILITY	229
Eco-Tourism and Sustainability	229
Eco-Friendly Accommodations	230
Top Eco-Friendly Resorts and Lodges in Thailand	231
Benefits of Staying in Eco-Friendly Accommodations	234
Tips for Identifying and Booking Eco-Friendly Stays	236

Responsible Wildlife Tourism	238
Principles of Responsible Wildlife Tourism	238
Ethical Wildlife Experiences in Thailand	240
The Impact of Responsible Wildlife Tourism	242
Tips for Ensuring Responsible Wildlife Interactions	244
Supporting Local Communities	246
The Importance of Supporting Local Communities	247
Community-Based Tourism Projects in Thailand	248
Benefits of Engaging in Community-Based Tourism	251
Tips for Responsibly Supporting Local Communities	253
CHAPTER 14: DETAILED SAMPLE ITINERARIES	256
Detailed Itineraries	256
One-Week Highlights Tour	256
Two-Week Cultural Immersion	260
One-Month Adventure and Relaxation	264
CHAPTER 15: PRACTICAL AND UP-TO-DATE TRAVEL ADVICE	268
Practical and Up-to-Date Travel Advice	268
Essential Packing Lists for Thailand	268
General Packing Checklist	269
Specialized Packing Lists for Different Traveler Types	270
Seasonal Packing Considerations	271
Practical Tips for Efficient Packing	272
Navigating Thai Healthcare and Emergencies	273
Overview of the Thai Healthcare System	274
Finding and Choosing Healthcare Facilities	275
Handling Medical Emergencies	276
Preventive Health Measures	277

Using Travel Apps and Online Resources	279
Essential Travel Apps for Navigating Thailand	279
Online Resources for Trip Planning	281
Social Media and Travel Communities	283
Tips for Staying Connected	285
CHAPTER 16: INSIDER TIPS FROM THAI LOCALS	288
Insider Tips from Thai Locals	288
The Value of Local Knowledge	288
Specific Tips from Thai Locals	290
Connecting with Locals: How to Engage for Deeper Insights	292
Stories of Meaningful Local Interactions	293
CONCLUSION	296
REVIEW	299
Enjoyed the Trip? Review the Guide!	299
REFERENCES	302
About the Author	304
Also by Wanderlust Wren	306

INTRODUCTION

Picture this: stepping off the plane in Thailand, the warm, tropical air wraps around you like a welcoming embrace. The excitement is electric, mixed with just a hint of nervousness. Imagine venturing into the bustling streets of Bangkok; the city's vibrant chaos will sweep you off your feet. Tuk-tuks zooming by in a blur, and the mouthwatering aroma of street food filled the air, pulling you in every direction. Research has only deepened my love for Thailand and sparked the idea for this guide. I couldn't wait to share the magic of this country with you and help you plan a bucket list trip!

This book is your ultimate travel buddy; here to make your first trip to Thailand as smooth as a mango smoothie. Whether itching to dive into the vibrant cities, chill on sun-soaked beaches, or immerse yourself in the rich, colorful culture, this guide has got you covered. It's designed to take the guesswork out of planning and turn your trip into a breezy, unforgettable adventure.

My vision for this book? Simple. I want you to feel the thrill and awe I did without stress. This guide is vital to unlocking Thailand's wonders, from the well-known to the wonderfully unexpected. I've packed it with practical tips, insider secrets, and budget-friendly hacks to ensure your trip isn't just possible—it's extraordinary. Whether searching for hidden treasures or trying to tick off those must-see sights, this book provides every moment of your journey with pure magic.

Who's this book for? It's for anyone with a spirit of adventure and a love for new experiences. Solo travelers ready to conquer the unknown, couples dreaming of a romantic escape, families looking to create lifelong memories, or travel junkies eager to dive into Thailand's rich culture—this guide is made with you in mind. If you're planning your first trip to Thailand, you're in the right place. I've crafted this book to be your go-to resource, packed with everything you need to create the perfect trip tailored just for you.

To keep things easy and breezy, I've organized this guide into bite-sized chapters that cover every angle of your trip. We'll start with the basics—planning, budgeting, and itinerary building—before diving into the fun stuff like navigating local transport, uncovering authentic experiences, and finding those hidden gems that will make your trip truly special. There's also plenty of advice on cultural etiquette, safety tips, outdoor adventures, and special sections for romantic getaways, family-friendly activities, and eco-tourism. Each chapter is packed with detailed itineraries, practical tips, and personal stories that will bring Thailand to life right before your eyes.

This guide is more than just travel tips—it's a treasure trove of insights from countless hours of researching Thailand, learning from local experts, and soaking up wisdom from seasoned travelers. Every piece of advice has been road-tested and handpicked to ensure it is spot-on, relevant, and ideally suited for first-time visitors like you.

By the time you turn the last page, you'll be raring to go, armed with everything you need to make your Thailand adventure a smashing success. You'll have the confidence to easily plan your trip, discover hidden gems that most tourists miss, and stretch your budget without skimping on experiences. This guide is your ticket to an unforgettable journey with memories you'll treasure forever.

So, what are you waiting for? Dive into this guide with a big smile and an open heart. Let's explore Thailand together! Whether you're getting lost in the lively markets, lounging on a picture-perfect beach, or soaking up history at ancient temples, this book is your trusty sidekick for a trip full of unforgettable moments. Your adventure starts right here—let's make it one for the books!

Thailand

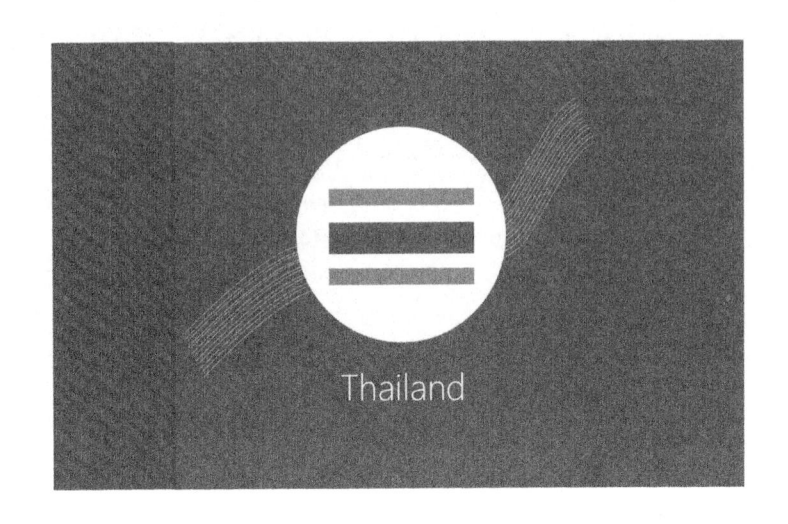

CHAPTER 1: UNDERSTANDING THAILAND

An Overview of Thailand's Geography and Climate

Welcome to the Land of Smiles, a country where diverse landscapes and climates create a travel experience like no other. Whether you're drawn to the misty mountains of the north, the bustling cities of the central plains, or the sun-drenched beaches of the south, Thailand offers something for every kind of traveler. Let's explore this fantastic country's geographical and climatic wonders to help you understand the lay of the land and plan your adventure accordingly.

The Geographical Layout of Thailand

Thailand's geography is as varied as its culture, with each region offering unique landscapes and experiences.

- **Northern Highlands:** In the north, you'll find the mountainous region, home to Thailand's tallest peaks and a rich tapestry of forests, waterfalls, and hill tribes. This area is perfect for trekking, cultural immersion, and exploring ancient cities like Chiang Mai and Chiang Rai. The cool, crisp air here provides a refreshing contrast to the tropical heat found elsewhere in the country.

- **Central Plains**: Often referred to as the "Rice Bowl of Asia," the central plains are a fertile and densely populated region, crisscrossed by rivers and dotted with bustling cities like Bangkok and Ayutthaya. This area is the heart of Thailand's agricultural industry and is known for its vibrant cities, historical sites, and the mighty Chao Phraya River, which flows through the heart of Bangkok.
- **Eastern Seaboard**: Moving east, you'll encounter Thailand's eastern seaboard, a coastal region famed for its beautiful beaches and islands, including the popular tourist destination of Pattaya and the tranquil island of Koh Samet. This region combines industrial hubs and serene coastal towns, blending modernity and natural beauty.
- **Southern Peninsular Region**: The southern part of Thailand is a narrow strip of land that extends into the Malay Peninsula, flanked by the Andaman Sea to the west and the Gulf of Thailand to the east. This region is famous for its stunning beaches, crystal-clear waters, and iconic islands like Phuket, Koh Samui, and the Phi Phi Islands. The south is also home to lush rainforests, limestone cliffs, and some of the country's best marine national parks.

Climate Variations Across the Regions

Thailand's climate is predominantly tropical, but it varies significantly across the different regions, which can greatly affect your travel plans.

- **Tropical Climate**: Thailand experiences three main seasons—hot, rainy, and cool.
- **Hot Season**: From March to June, temperatures soar, especially in the central and northern regions. This is an excellent time for beach lovers to hit the southern coasts.
- **Rainy Season**: Lasting from July to October, the monsoon season brings heavy rainfall, particularly to the western coast. Travel during this time can be unpredictable, but the lush green landscapes are a sight to behold.
- **Cool Season**: November to February is the best time to visit most of Thailand, especially the north. The temperatures are pleasantly cool, making it ideal for outdoor activities.
- **Monsoon Impacts**: The monsoon season affects the eastern and western coasts differently. The Andaman Sea (west coast) sees its rainy season peak from May to October, while the Gulf of Thailand (east coast) experiences more rain from October to January. This means that while one coast may be rainy, the other could enjoy dry, sunny weather—a crucial detail for beachgoers!

Key Geographical Features and Natural Landmarks

Thailand has various natural wonders, each offering a unique glimpse into the country's rich biodiversity and stunning landscapes.

- **Chao Phraya River**: Often referred to as Thailand's lifeblood, this river flows from the central plains down to the Gulf of Thailand. It's lined with historical sites, temples, and vibrant markets, making it a must-see for travelers to Bangkok.

- **Khao Sok National Park**: Located in the southern region, Khao Sok is one of Thailand's most beautiful national parks. It boasts ancient rainforests, towering limestone cliffs, and the breathtaking Cheow Lan Lake. It's a haven for nature lovers, offering opportunities for trekking, wildlife spotting, and overnight stays in floating bungalows.

- **Phi Phi Islands**: Famous for their dramatic cliffs, crystal-clear waters, and vibrant marine life, these islands in the Andaman Sea are a true paradise. They are perfect for snorkeling, diving, and simply soaking up the sun on pristine beaches.

Maps and Visual Aids

To help you visualize the geographical diversity and plan your trip more effectively, here are some maps:

- **Regional Map with Climate Zones**: This map highlights Thailand's five central regions and the different climatic zones to help you decide the best time to visit each area.

CHAPTER 1: UNDERSTANDING THAILAND

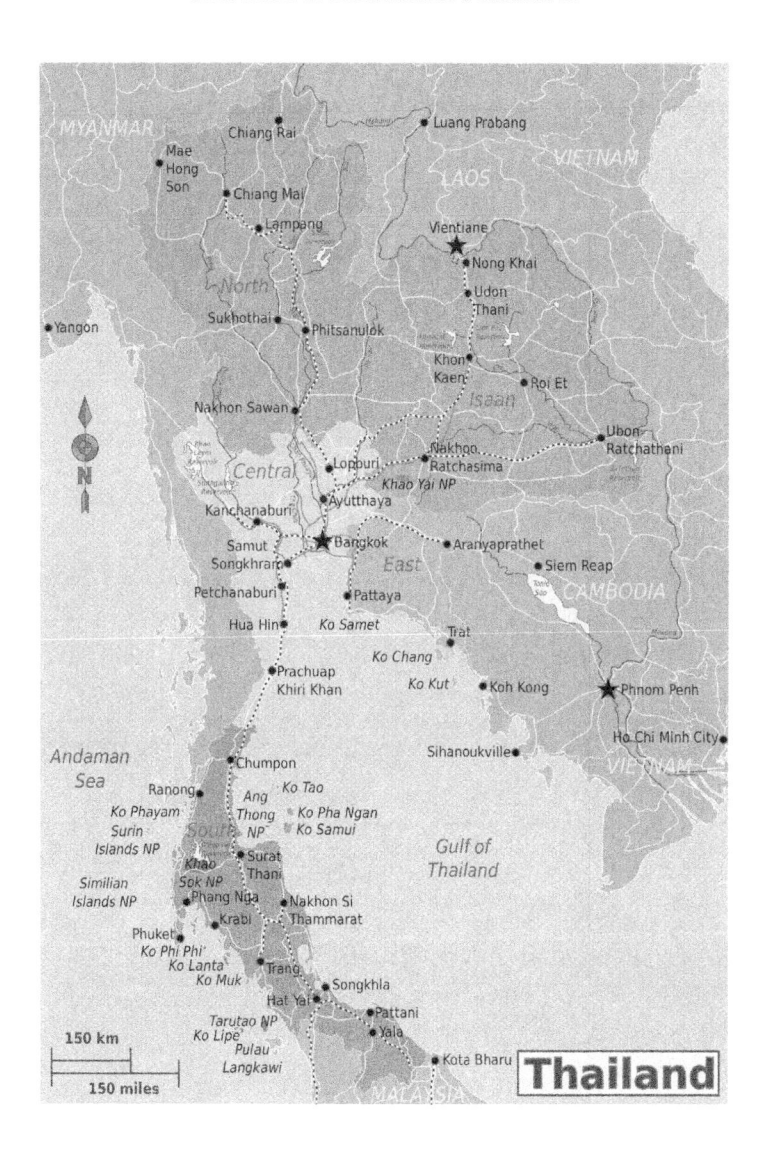

Major Tourist Destinations Map: This map marks the key

cities, beaches, and natural landmarks in Thailand, making it easier to plan your itinerary and make the most of your time there.

CHAPTER 1: UNDERSTANDING THAILAND

Understanding Thailand's geography and climate is the first

step in crafting a trip that suits your preferences, whether you're looking for adventure in the mountains, relaxation on the beach, or cultural exploration in the cities. With this knowledge, you're well on your way to experiencing all this incredible country offers.

CHAPTER 2: A BRIEF HISTORY OF THAILAND

To truly appreciate Thailand's vibrant culture and rich traditions, it's essential to delve into its fascinating history. Thailand's past is a tapestry woven with the rise and fall of kingdoms, the influence of powerful monarchs, and the country's resilient journey through various historical events. In this chapter, we'll walk through time, exploring the key milestones that have shaped Thailand into today's nation.

Ancient History and the Formation of Early Thai Kingdoms

Thailand's story begins with the establishment of early civilizations, which laid the foundation for the country's future.

Sukhothai Kingdom: The First Thai Kingdom

- The Sukhothai Kingdom, founded in the 13th century, is often considered the birthplace of Thai culture. This kingdom marked the first time the Thai people united under a single ruler, and it's credited with developing many aspects of Thai culture, including the Thai alphabet, which King Ramkhamhaeng created. Sukhothai is often revered as a golden age characterized by prosperity, artistic achievement, and the flourishing of Buddhism. Today, the remnants of this once-great kingdom can be explored at the Sukhothai Historical Park, where ancient temples and statues stand as a testament to its legacy.

Ayutthaya Kingdom: The Rise and Fall

- Following the decline of Sukhothai, the Ayutthaya Kingdom emerged in the 14th century and quickly became one of Southeast Asia's most powerful empires. Located strategically along the Chao Phraya River, Ayutthaya became a central trading hub, attracting merchants from Europe, China, and Japan. The kingdom was known for its grand architecture, numerous temples, and a rich cultural life. Unfortunately, Ayutthaya's glory ended in 1767 when it was sacked by Burmese invaders, leaving the city in ruins. The Ayutthaya Historical Park, with its crumbling temples and towering Buddha statues, offers visitors a glimpse into this once-mighty empire.

The Significance of the Chakri Dynasty

Thailand's history took a significant turn with the establishment of the Chakri Dynasty, which continues to rule today.

CHAPTER 2: A BRIEF HISTORY OF THAILAND

King Rama I: Founder of the Chakri Dynasty

- In 1782, following the fall of Ayutthaya, General Phra Phutthayotfa Chulalok (later known as King Rama I) established the Chakri Dynasty and moved the capital to Bangkok. Under his reign, the kingdom was stabilized, and Bangkok was transformed into a magnificent city by constructing the Grand Palace and Wat Phra Kaew (Temple of the Emerald Buddha). King Rama I also played a crucial role in preserving and codifying Thai laws, culture, and traditions, ensuring the continuity of the Thai identity.

The Current Monarchy: Role and Influence

- The Chakri Dynasty has continued to play a vital role in Thailand's development. The current monarch, King Maha Vajiralongkorn (King Rama X), ascended the throne in 2016 following the death of his father, King Bhumibol Adulyadej (King Rama IX), who was deeply loved and respected by the Thai people. While Thailand is now a constitutional monarchy, the royal family continues to hold significant influence and is regarded as a symbol of national unity and continuity.

Major Historical Events and Their Impact

Thailand's history is marked by several key events that have shaped its political and social landscape.

The 1932 Revolution: End of Absolute Monarchy

- One of the most pivotal moments in Thai history occurred in 1932 when a group of military officers and civil servants staged a coup, effectively ending the centuries-old absolute monarchy. This revolution led to a constitutional monarchy, where a constitution limited the king's powers. This shift marked the beginning of modern Thai politics and set the stage for the country's future development.

World War II: Thailand's Involvement

- During World War II, Thailand initially declared neutrality but later aligned with Japan after being invaded in 1941. Thailand became a strategic ally to Japan, allowing Japanese troops to pass through the country to invade British-controlled territories in Southeast Asia. After the war, Thailand managed to avoid severe repercussions due to its strategic negotiations with the Allies, thus maintaining its independence and sovereignty.

Treaty of Bowring: Opening of Thailand to International Trade

- The Treaty of Bowring, signed in 1855 between King Mongkut (Rama IV) and Britain, was a landmark event that opened Thailand (then known as Siam) to international trade. This treaty marked the beginning of Thailand's modernization, leading to increased foreign influence and the integration of Thailand into the global economy. The treaty also paved the way for establishing diplomatic relations with Western nations, ensuring Thailand's survival as the only Southeast Asian country never to be colonized.

Cultural and Historical Landmarks

Thailand's history is not just preserved in books—it's etched into the fabric of its cities and landscapes. Here are some must-visit historical landmarks that bring Thailand's past to life:

Ayutthaya Historical Park

- This UNESCO World Heritage Site is a sprawling complex of ancient temples, palaces, and statues that once formed the heart of the Ayutthaya Kingdom. Visitors can explore the ruins, including the iconic Wat Mahathat, where the famous Buddha's head is entwined in tree roots.

The Grand Palace in Bangkok

- A symbol of the Chakri Dynasty and the epicenter of Thai royal life, the Grand Palace is a must-see for any traveler to Bangkok. Within its walls, you'll find the Temple of the Emerald Buddha (Wat Phra Kaew), one of Thailand's most revered religious sites.

Sukhothai Historical Park

- This park is home to the ruins of the Sukhothai Kingdom, where visitors can marvel at the ancient temples and Buddha statues that date back to the 13th century. The park's serene atmosphere and historical significance make it a fascinating destination for history enthusiasts.

Thailand's rich history is a cornerstone of its identity, influencing everything from its culture and traditions to its modern-day politics. By exploring these historical milestones and landmarks, you'll gain a deeper understanding of the country and the people who call it home. Whether wandering through the ancient ruins of Ayutthaya or standing in awe at the Grand Palace, you're not just observing history—you're stepping into it.

CHAPTER 3: UNDERSTANDING THAI CULTURE AND TRADITIONS

Thailand is a country where ancient traditions and modern life blend seamlessly, creating a rich cultural tapestry that's as diverse as it is vibrant. To truly appreciate your journey through Thailand, it's essential to understand and respect the customs, traditions, and cultural norms that shape daily life here. In this chapter, we'll explore the critical aspects of Thai culture, delve into traditional practices, and provide practical tips to help you navigate social situations with ease and respect.

Critical Aspects of Thai Culture

Thai culture is deeply rooted in fundamental principles permeating every aspect of life, from family dynamics to religious practices.

Role of Buddhism: Temples and Monks

- Buddhism is the cornerstone of Thai culture, influencing everything from daily routines to national holidays. Approximately 95% of Thais practice Theravada Buddhism, and the country is dotted with thousands of temples known as *wats*. Monks, highly respected in Thai society, play a central role in religious and community life. Visitors to Thailand often see monks in saffron robes collecting alms in the early morning, which allows the community to earn merit. Temples serve as places of worship, meditation, and social gatherings, making them integral to Thai cultural life.

Wat Yai Chai Mongkon, Ayutthaya, Thailand

CHAPTER 3: UNDERSTANDING THAI CULTURE AND TRADITIONS

Family Structure: The Importance of Extended Family

- Family is the bedrock of Thai society, and the extended family is strongly emphasized. Unlike in many Western cultures, where nuclear families are more common, Thais often live in multi-generational households. Grandparents, parents, children, and sometimes even aunts, uncles, and cousins live together or nearby, supporting each other daily. Respect for elders is paramount, and decisions are often made considering the entire family's well-being. This substantial family structure is reflected in the way Thais interact with each other, emphasizing community over individuality.

Thai Respect and Etiquette: The Wai Gesture

- Respect is a core value in Thai culture, and it's often expressed through the *Wai*—a gesture made by pressing your palms together in a prayer-like position and bowing slightly. The *Wai* is a greeting, a sign of respect, and a way to thank you or apologize. The height at which you hold your hands and the depth of your bow indicate the level of respect you are showing, with higher hands and a more profound bow reserved for elders, monks, and people of higher social status. Understanding when and how to use the *Wai* is crucial for anyone wishing to engage respectfully in Thai society.

Traditional Thai Customs and Practices

Thailand's rich cultural heritage is showcased through its numerous festivals, ceremonies, and daily customs, many of which have been passed down through generations.

Songkran Festival: Thai New Year Water Festival

- One of the most famous Thai festivals, Songkran, marks the Thai New Year and is celebrated from April 13th to 15th. Originally a time for cleaning and renewal, Songkran has evolved into a nationwide water fight, with people taking to the streets to splash water on each other as a symbol of washing away the old year's bad luck. Despite the playful nature of the festival, Songkran is deeply rooted in tradition, with many people visiting temples to offer food to monks and pour water over Buddha statues as a form of reverence.

Loy Krathong: Festival of Lights

- Celebrated on the full moon night of the 12th lunar month, usually in November, Loy Krathong is a beautiful festival where people release floating baskets, known as *krathongs*, onto rivers and lakes. These baskets, often made from banana leaves and decorated with flowers, candles, and incense, are offerings to the water spirits and a way to pay respect to the Goddess of Water. The sight of thousands of illuminated krathongs drifting down the water is truly magical and offers a glimpse into the spiritual side of Thai culture.

Traditional Thai Weddings

- Thai weddings blend religious rituals and cultural traditions, with the ceremony often beginning with a Buddhist blessing by monks. One of the key elements of a traditional Thai wedding is the *rod nam sang* ritual, where the couple kneels together, and guests pour holy water over their hands while offering blessings. The wedding is also an opportunity for families to unite, celebrate, and support the newlyweds. The importance of community and family in Thai culture is evident in the warmth and joy of these celebrations.

Hands are pouring blessing water into the bride's hands, Thai wedding. Wedding ceremony in Thailand.

Cultural Norms and Etiquette for Travelers

Awareness of local customs and etiquette is essential to ensure a respectful and positive experience while visiting Thailand.

Temple Etiquette: Dress Code and Behavior

- When visiting temples, it's essential to dress modestly. This means covering your shoulders and knees and avoiding revealing clothing. Shoes must be removed before entering temple buildings, and it's polite to step over the threshold rather than on it. Inside the temple, keep your voice low, do not touch any religious objects, and never point your feet towards a Buddha statue or monk—this is considered extremely disrespectful.

Social Interactions: Do's and Don'ts

- When interacting with locals, it's essential to maintain a calm and polite demeanor. Thai values Sanuk (having fun) and mai pen rai (not worrying too much), which means maintaining a positive attitude is crucial. Avoid raising your voice or showing anger in public, as this can lead to a loss of face, which is a severe social faux pas. When giving or receiving something, it's polite to use both hands or your right hand while placing your left hand on your right forearm as a sign of respect.

CHAPTER 3: UNDERSTANDING THAI CULTURE AND TRADITIONS

Dining Etiquette: Use of Utensils and Communal Eating

- Dining in Thailand is a communal experience, with dishes typically shared among the group. It's customary to wait for the eldest person at the table to start eating first. Thais use a spoon and fork for most meals, with the spoon in the right hand and the fork in the left used to push food onto the spoon. Chopsticks are generally only used for noodle dishes. Leaving food on your plate is also considered polite, indicating you've had enough to eat.

The Diversity Within Thai Culture

While Thai culture has a strong sense of national identity, it's also incredibly diverse, with various ethnic groups and regions contributing to the cultural mosaic.

Hill Tribes in Northern Thailand

- The northern highlands of Thailand are home to several hill tribes, including the Karen, Hmong, and Akha people. These tribes have their distinct languages, customs, and traditional clothing, and they live in remote villages often visited by travelers interested in cultural tourism. The hill tribes are crucial in preserving this region's unique heritage and traditions.

Muslim Communities in Southern Thailand

- Southern Thailand has a significant Muslim population, particularly in the provinces bordering Malaysia. Islam's cultural influence is evident in the region's architecture, food, and festivals. Mosques are common, and visitors to these areas should be mindful of Islamic customs, including dressing modestly and respecting religious practices.

Chinese Influences in Urban Areas

- Chinese immigrants have significantly shaped Thailand's economy and culture, particularly in urban areas like Bangkok. Chinatown in Bangkok is a vibrant neighborhood where Chinese traditions, cuisine, and festivals are celebrated. The Chinese New Year is one of the city's most lively and colorful events, reflecting the deep-rooted Chinese influence in Thai society.

Understanding the intricacies of Thai culture and traditions will enhance your travel experience and allow you to connect more deeply with the people you meet along the way. By respecting local customs and embracing the diversity of Thai culture, you'll find your journey through Thailand to be richer, more meaningful, and full of unforgettable moments. Whether participating in a lively festival, visiting a serene temple, or simply sharing a meal with locals, these cultural insights will guide you in experiencing Thailand in its most authentic form.

CHAPTER 4: PLANNING YOUR TRIP

Planning a trip to Thailand can be as exciting as the journey itself. Whether you're dreaming of sun-soaked beaches, bustling cities, or serene temples, careful planning will help you make the most of your adventure. In this chapter, we'll guide you through the critical steps of planning your trip, from deciding when to visit to creating your ideal itinerary, ensuring you have a smooth and memorable experience in the Land of Smiles.

When to Visit Thailand: Best Times and Seasons

Thailand's tropical climate means that the weather can vary significantly throughout the year, and choosing the right time to visit can make a big difference in your travel experience. Here's a breakdown of the seasons to help you decide when to go.

Cool Season: November to February

- The cool season is Thailand's most popular time for visitors, with pleasant temperatures ranging from 20°C to 30°C (68°F to 86°F) across much of the country. This is the perfect time for outdoor activities, from exploring the temples of Bangkok to trekking in the northern mountains. However, as this is peak tourist season, be prepared for larger crowds and higher prices.

Hot Season: March to May

- The hot season sees temperatures soar, especially in central and northern Thailand, where they can reach up to 40°C (104°F). While the heat can be intense, this is an excellent time to visit the southern beaches, where the sea breeze offers relief. The hot season also means fewer tourists and lower prices, making it a fantastic option for budget travelers who can handle the heat.

Rainy Season: June to October

- The rainy or monsoon season brings heavy rains and high humidity. While the downpours can be intense, they're usually short-lived and followed by bright sunshine. The countryside is lush and green, making it a beautiful time for nature lovers. Additionally, there are fewer tourists, and you can often find great deals on accommodation and flights. Just be mindful that some areas, particularly in the south, may experience flooding.

Pros and Cons of Visiting During Each Season

Each season in Thailand offers its own unique advantages and challenges. Here's what you can expect:

Cool Season

- **Pros**: Pleasant weather, ideal for outdoor activities; vibrant festivals like Loy Krathong; excellent conditions for trekking and exploring.
- **Cons**: Higher prices for flights and accommodation; more crowded tourist spots; need to book in advance.

Hot Season

- **Pros**: Fewer tourists, which means less crowded attractions; great discounts on hotels and flights; perfect beach weather in the south.
- **Cons**: Intense heat, especially inland; limited activities due to high temperatures; some northern regions can be hazy from agricultural burning.

Rainy Season

- **Pros**: Lush landscapes, beautiful greenery, fewer tourists and lower prices, and the opportunity to experience Thailand's dramatic weather patterns.
- **Cons**: Heavy rain can disrupt travel plans; some islands and beaches may be less accessible; occasional flooding in certain regions.

Key Events and Festivals Throughout the Year

Thailand's calendar is filled with vibrant festivals and events that add a unique cultural dimension to your trip. Here are some highlights:

Songkran (Thai New Year) in April

- Songkran is Thailand's most famous festival, celebrated with water fights, temple visits, and traditional ceremonies. It's a joyous time to be in Thailand, particularly in cities like Bangkok, Chiang Mai, and Phuket. The water fights happen in the streets, and everyone is fair game: locals and tourists alike!

Crowd of people celebrating the traditional Songkran New Year Festival: Bangkok, Thailand

Loy Krathong in November

- Known as the Festival of Lights, Loy Krathong is one of Thailand's most beautiful festivals. People release small, decorated floats called krathongs onto rivers and lakes to pay respect to the water spirits. Chiang Mai and Sukhothai are especially magical places to experience this festival.

Chiang Mai Flower Festival in February

- This colorful event takes place in Chiang Mai, featuring parades, flower displays, and cultural performances. It's a beautiful way to experience the beauty of northern Thailand.

Chiang Mai, cultural experience

Recommendations Based on Traveler Preferences

Different types of travelers will find different seasons and events more appealing. Here's a quick guide to help you choose:

- **Family-friendly Seasons**: The cool season is ideal for families, with its mild weather and plenty of outdoor activities perfect for kids.
- **Best Time for Budget Travelers**: The hot season offers significant discounts on accommodation and flights, making it the best time for budget-conscious travelers.
- **Ideal Period for Adventure Activities**: The rainy season is perfect for those who love lush landscapes and don't mind a bit of rain during their trekking, rafting, or jungle adventures.

Essential Travel Documents and Preparations

Before you start your Thai adventure, please have all the necessary documents and preparations.

Passport Validity

- Your passport must be valid for at least six months beyond your planned stay in Thailand. Please make sure you have enough blank pages for entry and exit stamps.

Visa Requirements

- Depending on your nationality, you may need a visa to enter Thailand. Many travelers can use the visa exemption program, which allows up to 30 days of stay without a visa. Others may need to apply for a tourist visa in advance or obtain a visa on arrival for a fee. Check the latest visa requirements before you travel.

Health Preparations and Vaccinations

- Before traveling to Thailand, you should get vaccinations for Hepatitis A and Typhoid. You might also consider vaccinations for Rabies and Japanese Encephalitis, depending on your travel plans. Always use mosquito repellent to protect against mosquito-borne illnesses like Dengue fever, and be cautious with drinking water—stick to bottled water or water treated with a filtration system.

Travel Insurance

- Travel insurance is a must for any trip to Thailand. Ensure your policy covers medical expenses, emergency evacuation, and any adventure activities you plan to undertake, such as diving or trekking. Also, check that it includes coverage for trip cancellations, lost luggage, and other potential travel disruptions.

CHAPTER 4: PLANNING YOUR TRIP

Financial Preparations and Currency Exchange

- The currency in Thailand is the Thai Baht (THB). You can exchange money at banks, authorized exchange booths, or use widely available ATMs. Be aware that some ATMs charge a fee for foreign cards, so it's wise to withdraw larger amounts at once. Credit cards are accepted in most hotels and larger restaurants, but carrying cash for smaller purchases and in more rural areas is a good idea.

Essential Resources for Travelers to Thailand

When traveling to Thailand, it's crucial to be prepared with important resources, including emergency phone numbers, embassy information, and websites for visa requirements. Below is a comprehensive list of essential information that will help ensure your trip is safe and well-planned.

Emergency Phone Numbers

- **General Emergency Services** (Police, Ambulance, Fire): **191**
- **Tourist Police**: **1155**
- The Tourist Police are available 24/7 to assist foreign tourists with safety, security, and travel-related issues.
- **Ambulance and Medical Emergency**: **1669**
- **Marine Emergency** (Coastal Rescue): **1199**
- **Fire Brigade**: **199**

Embassy Information

Here are the details for some major embassies in Thailand:

United States Embassy in Bangkok

- **Address**: 120-122 Wireless Road, Lumpini, Pathumwan, Bangkok 10330, Thailand
- **Phone**: +66 2 205 4000
- **Emergency After-Hours**: +66 2 205 4000
- **Website:** https://th.usembassy.gov/

British Embassy in Bangkok

- **Address**: 14 Wireless Road, Lumpini, Pathumwan, Bangkok 10330, Thailand
- **Phone**: +66 2 305 8333
- **Emergency After-Hours**: +66 2 305 8333
- **Website**: https://www.gov.uk/world/organisations/british-embassy-bangkok

Canadian Embassy in Bangkok

- **Address**: 15th Floor, Abdulrahim Place, 990 Rama IV Road, Bangrak, Bangkok 10500, Thailand
- **Phone**: +66 2 646 4300
- **Emergency After-Hours**: +66 2 646 4300
- **Website**: https://www.international.gc.ca/country-pays/thailand-thailande/bangkok.aspx?lang=eng

Australian Embassy in Bangkok

- **Address**: 37 South Sathorn Road, Bangkok 10120, Thailand
- **Phone**: +66 2 344 6300
- **Emergency After-Hours**: +66 2 344 6300
- **Website**: https://thailand.embassy.gov.au/

Embassy of India in Bangkok

- **Address**: 46 Sukhumvit Road, Soi 23, Bangkok 10110, Thailand
- **Phone**: +66 2 258 0300-5
- **Emergency After-Hours**: +66 81 844 7556
- **Website**: https://embassyofindiabangkok.gov.in/

Visa Requirements and Information

For up-to-date visa information, travelers should check the official Thai government websites or their respective embassy's website. Here are some valuable resources:

Thai Ministry of Foreign Affairs:

- Ministry of Foreign Affairs - Visa Information
- https://www.mfa.go.th/en

Thai E-Visa Portal:

- Thai E-Visa Official Website: https://www.thaievisa.go.th/
- This portal allows travelers to apply for a visa online before arriving in Thailand.

Royal Thai Embassy or Consulate:

- Each country has its own Thai embassy or consulate, where travelers can find specific information about visa applications, including requirements, fees, and processing times.
- https://washingtondc.thaiembassy.org/en/index

Thailand Immigration Bureau:

- Thailand Immigration Bureau: https://www.immigration.go.th/
- This website provides detailed information on immigration policies, visa extensions, and other relevant legal matters for visitors.

This resource information will help you navigate any challenges you may encounter during your trip to Thailand, ensuring a smooth and enjoyable travel experience.

CHAPTER 4: PLANNING YOUR TRIP

Creating Your Ideal Itinerary

Crafting the perfect itinerary for your trip to Thailand depends on your interests, the length of your stay, and your preferred pace of travel. Here's how to get started.

Prioritizing Destinations and Activities

- **Must-see destinations:** Bangkok for its vibrant city life and temples; Chiang Mai for its cultural richness and mountainous surroundings; and Phuket for its beaches and island hopping.
- **Hidden Gems**: Pai, a laid-back town in the mountains; Koh Lanta, a quieter island with stunning beaches; Sukhothai, home to ancient ruins and historical significance.
- **Cultural Experiences**: To immerse yourself in the local culture, don't miss temple visits, exploring local markets, or taking a Thai cooking class.

Sample Itineraries for Different Trip Lengths

- **One-Week Itinerary**: Bangkok, Ayutthaya, and Chiang Mai. Experience Bangkok's energy, Ayutthaya's historic ruins, and Chiang Mai's cultural charm.
- **Two-Week Itinerary**: Bangkok, Chiang Rai, Pai, and Phuket. Dive deeper into northern Thailand's culture and end with relaxation on Phuket's beaches.
- **One-Month Itinerary**: Northern Thailand (Chiang Mai, Chiang Rai, Pai), Central Thailand (Bangkok, Ayutthaya),

and Southern Islands (Phuket, Koh Samui, Koh Tao). This allows you to fully explore Thailand's diverse regions leisurely.

Transportation Logistics and Time Management

- Domestic flights are the quickest way to travel between regions, with budget airlines offering affordable options. Trains and buses are more economical choices and provide a chance to see the countryside. In cities, tuk-tuks, *songthaews* (shared taxis), and regular taxis are common for getting around locally.

Tips on Flexibility and Spontaneous Travel

- While having a plan is sound, leaving some flexibility in your itinerary allows you to take spontaneous day trips, follow local advice, or adapt to weather changes. Keeping your schedule open can lead to unexpected adventures, whether it's a day trip from Bangkok to the floating markets or an unplanned beach day in Koh Samui.

Budget Travel Strategies

Thailand is known for being a budget-friendly destination, and with some careful planning, you can stretch your travel budget even further.

CHAPTER 4: PLANNING YOUR TRIP

Affordable Accommodation Options

- **Hostels**: Perfect for solo travelers and those on a tight budget, hostels offer dormitories and private rooms. For a reliable stay, look for popular chains like Lub d Hostels.
- **Guesthouses**: Often family-run, guesthouses throughout the country provide a more personal touch and offer basic but comfortable accommodations.
- **Budget Hotels**: Basic amenities and cleanliness are standard in budget hotels, making them a solid option for those seeking more privacy.
- **Home-stays**: For a more profound cultural experience, consider a homestay where you can live with a local family and immerse yourself in Thai life.

Getting the Best Deals on Accommodations

- Traveling during the off-season can significantly lower your costs. Booking in advance secures discounts, but don't overlook last-minute deals that can offer significant savings. If you're staying at a guesthouse, try negotiating prices, especially for longer stays.

Budget-Friendly Dining: Where to Eat Cheaply

- Street food is a cornerstone of Thai culture, offering delicious meals at unbeatable prices. Explore famous markets like Bangkok's Chinatown and Chiang Mai's Night Bazaar for a culinary adventure. Local food courts, such as those at Terminal 21 or MBK Center, provide options in a comfortable setting. To avoid tourist traps, seek out family-run restaurants or ask locals for their favorite spots. Sharing dishes is common in Thai dining and allows you to sample more of the cuisine without overspending.

Money-Saving Tips for Sightseeing and Activities

- Thailand's most iconic attractions, such as temples and public beaches, are free or affordable. Consider joining budget-friendly tours, such as walking tours in Bangkok's Old Town, or renting a bike to explore at your own pace. Purchasing discount passes, like the Bangkok City Pass, can help you save on multiple attractions. Don't forget to haggle at markets and watch for online deals on activities and experiences.

With careful planning, your trip to Thailand can be everything you've dreamed of and more. From choosing the best time to visit to crafting the perfect itinerary, this chapter has provided you with the tools and tips you need to prepare for an unforgettable adventure. Whether you're a seasoned traveler or embark on your first international trip, Thailand promises a journey filled with discovery, culture, and endless beauty.

CHAPTER 5: NAVIGATING THAILAND

Getting around Thailand is an adventure, with various transportation options catering to different travel styles and preferences. Whether navigating the bustling streets of Bangkok, traveling between cities, or exploring the countryside on a scooter, understanding how to use these modes of transport efficiently and safely will significantly enhance your travel experience. In this chapter, we'll guide you through the ins and outs of getting around Thailand, ensuring you're well-prepared for every leg of your journey.

Mastering Bangkok's Public Transportation

Bangkok's sprawling layout and heavy traffic can be daunting, but the city's public transportation system makes getting around surprisingly easy and efficient. Here's how to master the various modes of transport in the Thai capital.

BTS Sky train

- The BTS Sky train is a fast and convenient way to travel around Bangkok, especially during peak traffic hours. The Sky train covers two main lines: the Sukhumvit

Line and the Silom Line, which intersect at Siam Station, the heart of the city's shopping district. Tickets can be purchased from machines at each station, or you can get a Rabbit Card, a rechargeable smart card that makes travel more accessible. To avoid the crowds, try to travel outside peak hours (7:00-9:00 AM and 5:00-7:00 PM). The BTS is also wheelchair accessible, with elevators and ramps at most stations.

MRT Subway

- The MRT Subway complements the BTS by covering areas the Sky train doesn't reach. The Blue Line and the Purple Line are the main routes, with key interchange stations at Asok and Chatuchak Park connecting with the BTS. Like the BTS, tickets can be bought from machines or used with a stored-value card. The MRT is less crowded than the BTS during peak hours and is similarly accessible, with facilities for disabled travelers.

Public Buses

- Bangkok's public buses are a cheap and extensive way to get around, although they can be slower due to traffic. There are different types of buses: air-conditioned (blue or orange buses) and non-air-conditioned (red, blue, or white buses). Fares are low, typically ranging from 8 to 20 baht, depending on the bus type. You'll need an exact change to pay the bus conductor. Popular tourist routes include buses to the Grand Palace, Chatuchak Market, and Khao San Road. Apps like Moovit and ViaBus help

CHAPTER 5: NAVIGATING THAILAND

navigate the bus system.

Chao Phraya Express Boat

- For a scenic route through Bangkok, the Chao Phraya Express Boat offers a unique way to explore the city. These boats run up and down the Chao Phraya River, stopping at attractions such as Wat Arun, the Grand Palace, and Asiatique. There are different types of boats, including the Tourist Boat, which offers unlimited day passes, and the regular commuter boats, which are cheaper and more frequented by locals.

Detailed Guide to Using the BTS Sky Train and MRT Subway

Navigating the BTS and MRT systems is straightforward once you know the basics. Here's a step-by-step guide to help you move efficiently around Bangkok.

Buying Tickets

- You can purchase single-journey tickets from machines located at each station. These machines accept coins and banknotes, and instructions are available in English. Alternatively, the Rabbit Card (for BTS) or a stored-value card for the MRT allows you to skip the ticket queues. These cards can be topped up at any station and used for multiple trips.

Reading Maps and Interchange Points

- The BTS and MRT have clear route maps displayed at stations and inside trains. Interchange stations are well-marked, allowing you to switch between lines easily. For instance, Siam Station is the BTS Sukhumvit and Silom Lines interchange, while Asok (BTS) and Sukhumvit (MRT) stations connect the two systems.

Avoiding Peak Hours

- Bangkok's public transport can get crowded during peak hours. Plan your travel for mid-morning or early afternoon when the trains are less crowded. Alternatively, travel in the evening after the rush hour has subsided.

Accessibility

- Both the BTS and MRT are accessible to travelers with disabilities. Most stations have elevators, ramps, and designated seating areas. Station staff are generally helpful and can guide if needed.

Navigating the Bus System in Bangkok

While the bus system in Bangkok might seem complex, it's a cost-effective way to explore the city. Here's what you need to know.

Types of Buses

- Bangkok's buses range from basic, non-air-conditioned buses to more comfortable air-conditioned ones. The air-conditioned buses are typically blue or orange, while the non-air-conditioned ones are red, blue, or white. Fares are low, starting at around 8 baht, and vary depending on the type of bus and distance traveled.

Fare Payment

- Bus fares are collected by a conductor on the bus, so make sure you have small bills or exact change. If you're unsure of the fare, ask the conductor your destination, and they will tell you the cost.

Major Routes

- Some of the most useful bus routes for tourists include those heading to major attractions like the Grand Palace (bus 503), Chatuchak Market (bus 3), and Khao San Road (bus 15). For more detailed route planning, apps like Moovit or ViaBus can help you find the best bus routes and schedules.

Safety and Convenience Tips

- While public transport in Bangkok is generally safe, be mindful of your belongings, as pickpocketing can occur in crowded areas. If you're unfamiliar with the language, learning a few basic Thai phrases can be very helpful, or you can use translation apps like Google Translate. In case of emergencies or if you need assistance, keep the contact numbers for local support services handy.

Navigating Intercity Travel: Trains, Buses, and Flights

Traveling between cities in Thailand is easy, with various options to suit different budgets and preferences.

Train Travel Options

- Thailand's train system is a scenic and comfortable way to travel between major cities. There are three classes: first class (private cabins), second class (reclining seats or sleeping berths), and third class (basic seating). Popular routes include Bangkok to Chiang Mai and Bangkok to Surat Thani, the gateway to the southern islands. Tickets can be booked online through the State Railway of Thailand's website or purchased at railway stations. Overnight trains are popular for longer journeys, offering sleeper berths and dining car services.

Major Bus Companies and Routes

- Long-distance buses are another reliable option, with services ranging from VIP buses (with more comfort and amenities) to standard buses and minibusses. Major operators include Nakhonchai Air, and The Transport Co., Ltd. Tickets can be booked at bus terminals or online. Popular routes include Bangkok to Phuket and Chiang Mai to Pai. Buses are a budget-friendly travel method, with frequent departures and wide coverage nationwide.

Domestic Flights for Quick Travel

- Domestic flights are the fastest way to get around Thailand if time is of the essence. Budget airlines like Air Asia, Nok Air, and Thai Lion Air offer affordable fares, especially if booked in advance. Popular routes include Bangkok to Krabi and Chiang Mai to Phuket. Most major airports are well-connected by public transport or airport shuttles, making it easy to get to and from the airport.

Combining Different Modes of Transport

- To make the most of your trip, combine different modes of transport. For instance, you could take an overnight train from Bangkok to Surat Thani and catch a bus or ferry to Koh Samui. When you plan your itinerary, please make sure to allow for buffer times between connections to account for potential delays. Most major train stations and airports offer luggage storage facilities, making it easier to manage your belongings during multi-modal travel.

Renting Scooters and Bikes Safely

Renting a scooter or bike is a popular way to explore Thailand, especially the islands or the countryside. Here's how to do it safely and legally.

Renting Process

- To rent a scooter or bike, you must provide a valid ID, such as a passport and sometimes an international driving permit. Rental costs vary depending on the type of vehicle and rental period, but daily rates typically start at around 150-300 baht for scooters. Always read the rental agreement carefully and check that the vehicle is insured.

Safety Precautions and Riding Tips

- Safety should be your top priority when riding a scooter or bike. Always wear a helmet—this is not only for your safety but is also required by law. Familiarize yourself with Thailand's road rules, such as driving on the left and obeying speed limits. Defensive driving is crucial, especially in busy areas with unpredictable traffic. Avoid riding in heavy traffic or at night if you're not experienced.

Popular Destinations for Scooter and Bike Exploration

- Some of the best places to explore by scooter or bike include the Mae Hong Son Loop in Northern Thailand, a scenic route through mountains and valleys, and the coastal roads of Phuket and Koh Samui, where you can ride from beach to beach. For those looking to venture off the beaten path, the rural areas around Chiang Mai offer quiet roads and beautiful countryside.

Maintaining and Returning Rented Vehicles

- Before setting off, check your scooter or bike for any issues, such as tire pressure, brakes, and lights. Fueling stations are easy to find in most areas, and scooters typically use regular gasoline. If you have any problems with the vehicle, please let the rental company know as soon as possible.

CHAPTER 6: AUTHENTIC LOCAL EXPERIENCES

Experiencing Thai Festivals and Events

Thailand is a country that genuinely knows how to celebrate. Throughout the year, vibrant festivals and events light up the nation, offering travelers a unique and immersive glimpse into Thai culture, traditions, and community spirit. From nationwide water fights to serene lantern releases, these festivities are as diverse as they are captivating. This chapter will explore some of Thailand's most iconic festivals, delve into their rich histories and traditions, and provide essential tips for respectful and enjoyable participation. We'll also highlight some lesser-known regional celebrations that offer equally enchanting experiences off the typical tourist trail.

Major Thai Festivals

Thailand's calendar is filled with festivals that reflect its cultural diversity and deep-rooted traditions. Here are the four most celebrated events that attract local and international visitors.

Songkran: The Thai New Year Water Festival

Overview: Songkran is Thailand's most famous festival, marking the traditional Thai New Year. Celebrated annually from April 13th to 15th, Songkran transforms the entire country into a joyous, water-soaked playground where locals and tourists come together to welcome the new year with fun and festivity.

Celebrations:

- **Water Fights:** Streets across Thailand become arenas for friendly water battles. People armed with water guns, buckets, and hoses drench each other in a symbolic cleansing ritual to wash away misfortunes and welcome blessings for the coming year.
- **Temple Activities:** Many Thais visit temples to offer food to monks and participate in merit-making ceremonies. Pouring scented water over Buddha statues and the hands of elders is a common practice, symbolizing purification and respect.
- **Processions and Cultural Shows:** Colorful parades featuring traditional dances, music, and beautifully decorated floats are held in various cities, showcasing Thailand's rich cultural heritage.

Best Places to Celebrate:

- **Bangkok:** The capital hosts massive celebrations, particularly on Khao San Road and Silom Road, where energetic

crowds gather for nonstop water fun.
- **Chiang Mai:** Known for hosting some of the most elaborate Songkran festivities, including the famous procession of the revered Phra Phuttha Sihing Buddha image.
- **Phuket:** Beaches and streets come alive with water parties and lively entertainment, offering a tropical twist to the celebrations.

Loy Krathong: The Festival of Lights

Overview: Loy Krathong is one of Thailand's most enchanting festivals, celebrated on the full moon night of the 12th lunar month, usually in November. The name translates to "float a basket," reflecting the tradition of releasing beautifully decorated floats onto waterways to pay respect to the water goddess and seek forgiveness for past misdeeds.

Celebrations:

- **Floating Krathongs:** People gather by rivers, lakes, and canals to release lotus-shaped baskets made from banana leaves adorned with flowers, candles, and incense sticks. As the candles illuminate the water, the sight creates a mesmerizing and serene atmosphere.
- **Fireworks and Light Displays:** The night sky is often lit with spectacular fireworks and lanterns, adding to the magical ambiance.
- **Cultural Performances:** Traditional dances, music, and beauty contests known as "Noppamas Queen Contests" are held nationwide.

Best Places to Celebrate:

- **Sukhothai:** Considered the birthplace of Loy Krathong, Sukhothai Historical Park hosts grand celebrations with stunning light and sound shows amid ancient ruins.
- **Chiang Mai:** The festival coincides with Yi Peng, creating a combined spectacle of floating baskets and sky lanterns.
- **Bangkok:** Festivities along the Chao Phraya River, particularly near Asiatique and the Rama VIII Bridge, offer breathtaking views and lively entertainment.

Yi Peng: The Lantern Festival in Chiang Mai

Overview: Yi Peng is a northern Thai festival celebrated concurrently with Loy Krathong, predominantly in Chiang Mai. The festival is renowned for its awe-inspiring sight of thousands of illuminated lanterns floating gracefully into the night sky, symbolizing the release of misfortunes and the welcoming of good luck.

Celebrations:

- **Releasing Sky Lanterns:** Participants light and release lanterns called "khom loi," creating a celestial spectacle that's both peaceful and uplifting.
- **Parades and Cultural Shows:** The streets of Chiang Mai feature vibrant processions, traditional Lanna dances, and elaborate decorations.
- **Temple Ceremonies:** Locals visit temples to make merit, offer prayers, and participate in Buddhist rituals.

Key Events:

- **Mae Jo Lantern Release:** This mass lantern release event often occurs at Mae Jo University and attracts thousands of visitors. It is usually a paid and organized event that requires advance booking.
- **Tha Phae Gate Celebrations:** Central Chiang Mai hosts free public events, including lantern releases, food stalls, and performances.

Phi Ta Khon: The Ghost Festival in Loei Province

Overview: Phi Ta Khon is a unique and colorful festival celebrated in the Dan Sai district of Loei Province, typically in June or July. The Ghost Festival combines religious traditions, playful ceremonies, and vibrant parades, reflecting the community's local legends and Buddhist beliefs.

Celebrations:

- **Costumed Parades:** Participants dress in elaborate, spooky ghost masks made from carved coconut tree trunks and rice husks, accompanied by flamboyant costumes. They dance and parade through the streets, creating a lively, whimsical atmosphere.
- **Rocket Launches:** Homemade rockets are launched to encourage rainfall for the upcoming farming season.
- **Buddhist Ceremonies:** The festival includes merit-making activities, sermons, and processions honoring the Buddhist story of Prince Vessantara's return, which is central to the festival's origin.

Unique Aspects:

CHAPTER 6: AUTHENTIC LOCAL EXPERIENCES

- **Community Participation:** The local community gets involved, showcasing traditional music, dances, and crafts.
- **Cultural Fusion:** The festival blends animist and Buddhist practices, reflecting Thailand's diverse spiritual landscape.

Visiting Tips:

- **Timing:** The exact dates vary yearly, so please check local schedules beforehand.
- **Accommodation:** Book early as the small town attracts many visitors during the festival.

History and Traditions Behind Each Festival

Understanding the origins and significance of these festivals enhances appreciation and allows for deeper cultural engagement.

Songkran's Origins: Ancient Purification Rituals

- **Historical Roots:** Songkran has its roots in ancient Hindu and Buddhist traditions, marking the solar calendar's new year.
- **Purification and Renewal:** Water symbolizes cleansing and renewal. Traditionally, water was gently poured over Buddha images and elders' hands to show respect and wash away bad luck.
- **Modern Evolution:** Over time, the ritual has transformed into the playful water fights seen today, but the

underlying themes of renewal, respect, and community remain central.

Loy Krathong: Honoring the Water Goddess

- **Historical Significance:** Loy Krathong is believed to have originated from Brahmin rituals and was later adapted into Thai culture to honor Phra Mae Khongkha, the Goddess of Water.
- **Symbolism:** Releasing the Krathong represents letting go of grudges, anger, and negative thoughts, paying respect, and seeking forgiveness for using and polluting the water.
- **Traditional Elements:** Many people include strands of hair, nail clippings, or coins in their krathongs as offerings and symbols of casting away misfortunes.

Yi Peng's Significance: Letting Go of Misfortunes

- **Lanna Tradition:** Yi Peng is rooted in the ancient Lanna Kingdom's traditions, which are celebrated primarily in northern Thailand.
- **Lantern Symbolism:** The act of releasing lanterns into the sky signifies letting go of past troubles and inviting good fortune. It also pays homage to Buddha and spreads merit.
- **Spiritual Undertones:** The festival is a time for meditation, reflection, and making merit through acts of kindness and charity.

CHAPTER 6: AUTHENTIC LOCAL EXPERIENCES

Phi Ta Khon's Roots: Buddhist Folklore and Local Legends

- **Legendary Origins:** The festival is inspired by a Buddhist tale where Prince Vessantara, a previous incarnation of Buddha, returns from a long journey. His return was so joyous that even the spirits came out to celebrate.
- **Animist Influences:** The ghostly costumes and masks reflect local animist beliefs and the community's connection to the spirit world.
- **Cultural Preservation:** The festival serves to preserve and pass down local folklore, traditions, and communal identity through generations.

Tips for Participating Respectfully

Engaging in Thai festivals is a rewarding experience, but it's important to do so respectfully to honor local customs and traditions.

Dress Appropriately

- **Modest Clothing:** Regardless of the festival, wearing modest clothing is appreciated. Covering shoulders and knees is especially important during religious ceremonies and temple visits.
- **Traditional Attire:** Embracing traditional Thai clothing can enhance your experience and show respect. Many locals wear traditional garments during Loy Krathong and Yi Peng, and tourists are welcome to do the same.
- **Practical Considerations:**
- **Songkran:** Wear lightweight, quick-drying clothes and

waterproof footwear. Avoid wearing white or transparent fabrics.

- **Phi Ta Khon:** Comfortable clothing and shoes are advisable as you'll likely be walking and standing for extended periods.

Behavioral Etiquette

- **Respect Rituals:** Observe and respect all religious and cultural rituals. Follow the locals' lead and participate when appropriate.
- **Mindful Conduct:** Avoid excessive drinking, rowdy behavior, and disrespectful actions, especially in sacred spaces.
- **Photography:** Always ask for permission before photographing individuals, particularly monks, and participants in ceremonial roles.

Safety Tips

- **Songkran:**
- **Protect Valuables:** Use waterproof bags or pouches to protect phones, cameras, and important documents.
- **Stay Hydrated:** The festival occurs during Thailand's hottest month; drink plenty of water and take breaks as needed.
- **Be Cautious:** Be mindful of water thrown forcefully and avoid participating in moving vehicles to prevent accidents.
- **Loy Krathong and Yi Peng:**
- **Handle Fire Carefully:** Exercise caution when lighting

and releasing lanterns or krathongs to prevent burns and accidental fires.
- **Environmental Consideration:** Use Eco-friendly materials for krathongs and ensure lanterns are released in designated areas.
- **Phi Ta Khon:**
- **Crowd Awareness:** Stay aware of your surroundings in crowded areas to avoid pick-pocketing and getting lost.
- **Weather Preparedness:** The festival often occurs during the rainy season; carry umbrellas or raincoats as needed.

Engaging with Local Customs

- **Participate Actively:** Join in traditional activities such as offering alms to monks, creating krathongs, or dancing alongside locals when invited.
- **Learn Basic Phrases:** Simple Thai greetings and expressions of gratitude can enhance interactions and show respect.
- **Support Local Vendors:** Purchase food, crafts, and souvenirs from local artisans to contribute to the community and economy.

Regional Variations and Lesser-Known Festivals

Beyond the major festivals, Thailand hosts numerous regional celebrations that offer unique and intimate cultural experiences.

Boon Bang Fai: The Rocket Festival in Yasothon

Overview: Held annually in May in the northeastern province of Yasothon, Boon Bang Fai is a lively festival where locals launch homemade rockets into the sky to encourage rainfall and ensure a fruitful rice-growing season.

Highlights:

- **Rocket Launches:** Elaborately crafted rockets, some reaching impressive sizes, are launched amid cheers and excitement.
- **Parades and Performances:** The festival features colorful processions, traditional dances, music, and beauty contests.
- **Festive Atmosphere:** Expect lots of fun, with locals indulging in food, drink, and merriment throughout the celebrations.

Visiting Tips:

- **Safety First:** Observe launches from designated safe areas and follow local guidance.
- **Engage Locally:** Interact with locals to learn more about the significance and craftsmanship behind the rockets.

Vegetarian Festival: Spiritual Purification in Phuket

Overview: The Vegetarian Festival, or "Tesagan Gin Je," is a nine-day event held in October, primarily in Phuket, celebrated by the Chinese community to promote spiritual cleansing and merit-making through a strict vegetarian diet

CHAPTER 6: AUTHENTIC LOCAL EXPERIENCES

and ritualistic ceremonies.

Highlights:

- **Street Processions:** Participants perform extreme acts of self-mortification, such as piercing their cheeks with sharp objects believed to bring good luck and drive away evil spirits.
- **Temple Ceremonies:** Numerous rituals, including fire-walking and bladed-ladder climbing, are performed at Chinese temples across Phuket.
- **Culinary Experience:** The streets are lined with stalls offering various delicious vegetarian and vegan dishes, providing a feast for food enthusiasts.

Visiting Tips:

- **Respectful Observation:** While the processions can be intense, observe respectfully and avoid obstructing participants.
- **Dietary Participation:** Embrace the festival's spirit by sampling and enjoying the diverse vegetarian cuisine available.
- **Dress Code:** Wear white clothing, which symbolizes purity and is customary during the festival.

Surin Elephant Round-Up: Celebrating the Majestic Elephants

Overview: Taking place annually in November in Surin Province, this festival honors the deep bond between the local people and elephants, showcasing the animals' strength, intelligence, and importance in Thai culture.

Highlights:

- **Elephant Performances:** Spectacular shows featuring elephants demonstrating traditional logging techniques, battle reenactments, and playful activities.
- **Elephant Buffet:** A grand feast is laid out for the elephants, creating a vibrant and joyful scene.
- **Cultural Shows:** Traditional dances, music, and parades complement the elephant performances, highlighting local arts and traditions.

Visiting Tips:

- **Ethical Considerations:** Ensure that interactions and activities are ethical and do not harm or exploit the elephants.
- **Advance Booking:** The festival is great, so please arrange accommodations and tickets beforehand.

CHAPTER 6: AUTHENTIC LOCAL EXPERIENCES

Thailand's Elephant Round-Up

Candle Festival in Ubon Ratchathani: Illuminating Artistry

Overview: Celebrated in July to mark the beginning of the Buddhist Lent, the Candle Festival in Ubon Ratchathani showcases intricate and enormous candle sculptures paraded through the city, highlighting exceptional craftsmanship and religious devotion.

Highlights:

- **Candle Processions:** Magnificent candles carved into elaborate designs and scenes from Buddhist mythology are displayed on floats accompanied by traditional dances and music.

- **Art Exhibitions:** Workshops and exhibitions demonstrate the candle carving process, offering insight into the artistry involved.
- **Nightly Festivities:** The city comes alive with light displays, cultural performances, and local markets.

Visiting Tips:

- **Timing:** Arrive a few days early to witness the candle preparations and carving competitions.
- **Cultural Engagement:** Participate in workshops and interact with artisans to deepen your appreciation of the craft.

Thailand's festivals and events offer unparalleled opportunities to immerse yourself in the country's rich cultural tapestry. Whether you're splashing through the streets during Songkran, releasing lanterns into the starry skies of Chiang Mai, or marveling at the artistry of Ubon Ratchathani's candle sculptures, these celebrations provide unforgettable experiences that capture the heart and soul of Thailand—understanding these festivals' history, traditions, and proper etiquette allows you to participate respectfully and meaningfully, forging deeper connections with the local culture and people. As you plan your journey, consider timing your visit to coincide with one or more of these vibrant events, and prepare to be swept away by the joy, color, and spirit that define Thailand's festive landscape.

CHAPTER 6: AUTHENTIC LOCAL EXPERIENCES

Exploring Local Markets and Street Food

One of the best ways to experience the heart and soul of Thailand is by immersing yourself in its vibrant local markets and indulging in the delicious array of street food. Markets are not just places to shop; they are cultural hubs where you can witness the daily life of locals, discover unique handicrafts, and savor the flavors that define Thai cuisine. Now we will take you on a journey through Thailand's bustling markets, guide you to the must-visit spots, and introduce you to the street food delights that you simply can't miss.

The Concept of Local Markets in Thailand

Thailand's markets are an integral part of daily life. They offer everything from fresh produce and clothing to handmade crafts and delectable street food. Each market has its own distinct atmosphere, making every visit a new adventure.

Types of Markets:

- **Floating Markets:** These markets are typically found along rivers and canals, where vendors sell goods directly from their boats. They offer a unique shopping experience and a glimpse into traditional Thai river life.
- **Night Markets:** Night markets come alive after the sun sets, offering a mix of food, fashion, and entertainment. They are perfect for those who enjoy browsing stalls under the glow of market lights, with the added bonus of live music and street performances.
- **Weekend Markets:** These markets are usually larger and more diverse, catering to both locals and tourists.

They operate mainly on Saturdays and Sundays, offering everything from antiques to trendy fashion items.
- **Market Layout:** Most Thai markets are organized into distinct sections, with stalls selling similar items grouped together. You'll often find separate areas for clothing, food, and crafts, with a dedicated food court or street food section where you can sit down and enjoy a meal.

Floating Market: Bangkok

Popular Markets:

- **Chatuchak Weekend Market (Bangkok):** One of the largest markets in the world, Chatuchak offers over

15,000 stalls selling everything imaginable, from vintage clothing to exotic pets. It's a must-visit for serious shoppers and casual browsers alike.
- **Damnoen Saduak Floating Market (Ratchaburi):** The most famous of Thailand's floating markets, Damnoen Saduak, offers a colorful and photogenic shopping experience. Vendors paddle their boats along the narrow canals, selling fresh fruits, souvenirs, and snacks.

Must-Visit Markets for Unique Experiences

While Thailand has countless markets, some stand out for their unique atmosphere and cultural significance. Here are a few you shouldn't miss.

Amphawa Floating Market (Samut Songkhram):

- **Overview:** Unlike the more touristy Damnoen Saduak, Amphawa Floating Market has a more local feel and operates mainly in the late afternoon and evening. It's famous for its grilled seafood, which vendors prepare directly on their boats.
- **Unique Experiences:** After shopping and dining, you can take a boat tour to see the fireflies along the riverbanks—a magical experience that sets this market apart.

Chiang Mai's Sunday Walking Street (Chiang Mai):

- **Overview:** Chiang Mai's old city comes alive every Sunday with a vibrant walking street market. The entire length of Ratchadamnoen Road is closed to traffic, allowing vendors to set up stalls selling handmade crafts, clothes, and local delicacies.
- **Unique Experiences:** In addition to shopping, you can enjoy street performances and live music and sample northern Thai specialties like Khao Soi.

Talad Rot Fai (Bangkok):

- **Overview:** Also known as the Train Market, Talad Rot Fai is a vintage-themed market that's a treasure trove for retro lovers. It's located on Srinakarin Road and offers various vintage items, from antique furniture to quirky collectibles.
- **Unique Experiences:** The market is also famous for its food stalls and bars, making it a great place to hang out in the evening.

Warorot Market (Chiang Mai):

- **Overview:** Warorot Market, also known as Kad Luang, is a traditional market in Chiang Mai where locals shop for everything from fresh produce to textiles. It's a great place to experience authentic northern Thai culture.
- **Unique Experiences:** The market is particularly famous for its selection of northern Thai foods, including Sai Oua (northern Thai sausage) and Nam Prik Ong (chili dip).

Popular Street Food Dishes and Where to Find Them

Thailand is a street food paradise, with a seemingly endless variety of dishes to try. Here's a guide to some of the must-try street food items and where to find them.

Pad Thai:

- **Description:** Pad Thai is Thailand's most famous dish. It consists of stir-fried rice noodles with eggs, tofu, shrimp or chicken, bean sprouts, and peanuts, all seasoned with tamarind paste and lime.
- **Where to Find It:** While Pad Thai is available everywhere, some of the best can be found on Bangkok's Khao San Road and in the street stalls of Thip Samai, widely considered one of the best Pad Thai vendors in Bangkok.

Pad-Thai

Som Tum (Spicy Papaya Salad):

- **Description:** This spicy salad is made from shredded green papaya, tomatoes, peanuts, dried shrimp, and chili, pounded with a mortar and pestle. It's a staple of Isaan cuisine, known for its intense flavors.
- **Where to Find It:** Som Tum is best enjoyed at local street stalls throughout the Isaan region and Bangkok's Silom and Sukhumvit areas.

CHAPTER 6: AUTHENTIC LOCAL EXPERIENCES

Som-Tum

Mango Sticky Rice:

- **Description:** A beloved Thai dessert, Mango Sticky Rice features sweet sticky rice topped with ripe mango slices and drizzled with coconut milk.
- **Where to Find It:** Mango sticky rice is available at most street food markets, particularly in Bangkok's Sukhumvit area and Chiang Mai's night markets.

Satay:

- **Description:** Satay is a popular snack across Southeast Asia. It consists of skewered and grilled meat, typically served with peanut sauce and a side of cucumber salad.
- **Where to Find It:** Satay can be found at most night markets, with some of the best in Bangkok's Talad Rot Fai and the markets in Phuket.

Satay

Khao Soi:

- **Description:** A northern Thai specialty, Khao Soi is a rich coconut curry noodle soup topped with crispy

noodles, pickled mustard greens, and a squeeze of lime. It's a must-try when visiting Chiang Mai.
- **Where to Find It:** Chiang Mai's Sunday Walking Street and Warorot Market are excellent places to try authentic Khao Soi.

Tips for Exploring Markets and Street Food Safely

While exploring markets and enjoying street food in Thailand is generally safe, a few precautions will help ensure a positive experience.

Food Safety Tips:

- **Choose Busy Stalls:** High turnover means the food is likely fresh. Look for stalls with many local customers, which is usually a good quality indicator.
- **Avoid Raw Items:** Unless you know the source, it's best to avoid raw or undercooked foods, particularly seafood, to minimize the risk of foodborne illness.
- **Stay Hydrated:** Walking around markets can be hot work, so drink plenty of water. Bottled water is readily available, and it's advisable to avoid tap water.

Bargaining Tips:

- **How to Haggle Politely:** Bargaining is common in Thai markets, but it should be done with a smile and a friendly attitude. Start by offering 50-60% of the asking price and negotiate from there.
- **When to Accept Prices:** If you feel the price is fair or the

vendor seems unwilling to negotiate further, accepting the final price is respectful rather than pushing too hard.

Personal Safety:

- **Keep Belongings Secure:** Markets can get crowded, making them a prime pick-pocket spot. Keep your valuables secure, ideally in a money belt or an anti-theft bag.
- **Avoiding Crowded Areas:** If a market becomes too crowded, it is best to move to a less congested area to prevent the risk of theft or accidents.

Best Times to Visit:

- **Early Mornings:** For the freshest produce and a more relaxed shopping experience, visit markets early in the morning. This is also when vendors are most likely to offer the best prices.
- **Evenings:** Night markets are best visited in the evening when the atmosphere is lively and the street food stalls are in full swing.

Exploring Thailand's local markets and sampling its street food is a highlight of any visit to the country. Whether you're haggling for a unique souvenir, savoring a plate of Pad Thai, or simply soaking in the vibrant atmosphere, these experiences offer a genuine taste of Thai culture. By following the tips in this chapter, you can enjoy these markets and street food stalls safely and respectfully, ensuring that your journey through Thailand's culinary and cultural landscape is as rewarding as it is delicious.

Village Home-stays and Community Tours

For travelers seeking an authentic, immersive experience in Thailand, village homestays and community tours offer a unique opportunity to connect with the local culture on a deeper level. These experiences go beyond typical sightseeing, allowing you to live with local families, participate in traditional activities, and contribute to sustainable tourism efforts. In this section, we'll explore the benefits of choosing a homestay or community tour, recommend some of the best options across Thailand, describe the activities you can expect, and provide tips to help you prepare for an unforgettable stay.

The Benefits of Village Home-stays and Community Tours

Village homestays and community tours offer travelers a chance to experience real Thailand, far from the bustling cities and popular tourist spots. Here are some of the key benefits of choosing this type of experience.

Cultural Immersion:

- **Living with Local Families:** A village homestay allows you to live with a local family and experience their daily life firsthand. This includes participating in household activities, sharing meals, and learning about customs and traditions that are often passed down through generations.

- **Participating in Daily Activities:** Homestays often involve engaging in the village's daily routines, such as farming, cooking, or crafting. This hands-on involvement provides a deeper understanding of the local way of life and creates a more meaningful travel experience.

Sustainable Tourism:

- **Supporting Local Economies:** By staying in a village homestay or joining a community tour, you contribute directly to the local economy. The money you spend goes to the families and communities hosting you rather than large corporations, helping sustain traditional homestay lifestyles.
- **Minimizing Environmental Impact:** Many village homestays focus on Eco-tourism, promoting practices that minimize environmental impact, such as organic farming and sustainable resource use.

Educational Experiences:

- **Learning Traditional Crafts:** Home-stays often include workshops for traditional crafts such as weaving, pottery, or textile making. These activities provide insight into the skills and artistry that have been part of Thai culture for centuries.
- **Cooking and Agriculture:** Whether you learn to cook local dishes or help with rice planting and harvesting, these experiences are educational and deeply rewarding, offering a hands-on connection to the land and its people.

CHAPTER 6: AUTHENTIC LOCAL EXPERIENCES

Personal Connections:

- **Building Relationships with Local Hosts:** One of the most rewarding aspects of a homestay is the personal connections you make with your hosts. These relationships often transcend the language barrier, creating bonds based on shared experiences and mutual respect.

Recommended Village Home-stays and Community Tours

Thailand offers homestays and community tours, each providing a unique glimpse into the country's rich cultural tapestry. Here are some highly recommended options.

Ban Mae Kampong (Near Chiang Mai):

- **Overview:** Nestled in the mountains about an hour's drive from Chiang Mai, Ban Mae Kampong is a picturesque hill tribe village known for its Eco-tourism efforts. The village is surrounded by lush forests and tea plantations, making it a serene retreat.
- **Activities:** Visitors can participate in tea harvesting, traditional massage, and forest trekking. The village also offers cooking classes where you can learn to prepare local northern Thai dishes.

Lisu Lodge (Lisu Hill Tribe Experience):

- **Overview:** Located in the hills north of Chiang Mai, Lisu Lodge offers an immersive experience with the Lisu hill tribe. The lodge is part of a community-based tourism project that supports local conservation and cultural preservation efforts.
- **Activities:** Guests can enjoy cultural performances, guided walks through the village and surrounding countryside, and workshops on traditional Lisu crafts. They can also explore nearby temples and waterfalls.

Baan Tong Luang (Multi-Tribe Village):

- **Overview:** Situated near Chiang Mai, Baan Tong Luang is a cultural village that brings together various hill tribes, including the Karen, Hmong, and Lahu. It's a great place to learn about the diverse cultures and traditions of these different ethnic groups.
- **Activities:** Visitors can watch traditional weaving, visit the village's craft market, and participate in cultural exchange programs. The village also offers homestay options, where they can stay with a local family.

Koh Yao Noi (Island Home-stays):

- **Overview:** Located between Phuket and Krabi, Koh Yao Noi is a peaceful island known for its community-based tourism. The island's homestays offer a chance to experience the daily life of a fishing village away from the tourist crowds.

- **Activities:** Guests can join fishing trips, learn to cook southern Thai cuisine, and explore the island's natural beauty through guided hikes and bike tours. The island is also known for its traditional batik workshops.

Typical Activities and Experiences Offered

During your stay at a village homestay, you'll have the opportunity to engage in various activities that reflect the local culture and way of life. Here's what you can typically expect.

Traditional Cooking Classes:

- **Overview:** Learn to prepare local dishes using fresh ingredients from the village's gardens or nearby markets. These cooking classes often occur in the host family's kitchen, providing an intimate setting to learn culinary skills passed down through generations.
- **Example Dishes:** Depending on the region, you might learn to make dishes like Khao Soi in the north, Som Tum in the Isaan region, or Tom Yum in the south.

Traditional Thai Dish: Egg-Net

Craft Workshops:

- **Overview:** Participate in workshops to learn traditional crafts such as weaving, pottery, and textiles. These workshops teach you new skills and help preserve these important cultural practices.
- **Example Crafts:** You might learn to weave intricate patterns using a traditional loom, create pottery using local clay, or dye textiles using natural dyes.

Agricultural Activities:

- **Overview:** Get your hands dirty by joining in the village's agricultural activities, such as rice planting, harvesting, or organic farming. These experiences offer a deep connection to the land and the rhythms of rural life.
- **Seasonal Activities:** Depending on the time of year, you might participate in planting rice in the paddies, harvesting tea leaves, or helping with the seasonal fruit harvest.

Cultural Performances:

- **Overview:** Many villages offer cultural performances as part of the homestay experience. These can include traditional music and dance, storytelling, and even participation in local festivals.
- **Interactive Elements:** Guests are often invited to join in the performances, whether by learning a traditional dance, playing local musical instruments, or simply sitting around a fire listening to stories.

Tips for Choosing and Preparing for a Home-stay

Choosing a suitable homestay and preparing adequately can make all the difference in your experience. Here are some tips to help you get the most out of your village homestay.

Researching Options:

- **Read Reviews:** Before booking a homestay, read reviews from other travelers to understand what to expect. Look for homestays for their authenticity, hospitality, and activities offered.
- **Contacting Hosts:** Don't hesitate to contact the homestay or tour operator directly to ask questions or clarify details about the experience. This can help you gauge the level of communication and hospitality you can expect.

Packing Essentials:

- **Modest Clothing:** Villages often adhere to traditional and modest dress codes, so pack clothing that covers your shoulders and knees. Lightweight, breathable fabrics are ideal for the warm climate.
- **Gifts for Hosts:** Bringing a small gift for your host family is a thoughtful gesture that is greatly appreciated. Consider something from your home country, such as snacks, souvenirs, or handmade crafts.

Cultural Sensitivity:

- **Learning Basic Phrases:** Knowing a few basic Thai phrases or words in the local dialect can go a long way in building rapport with your hosts. Common greetings, thank yous, and polite expressions are especially useful.
- **Respecting Customs:** Familiarize yourself with local customs and etiquette before your stay. This includes practices around eating, dressing, and interacting with

CHAPTER 6: AUTHENTIC LOCAL EXPERIENCES

elders. Respect for local traditions will help you integrate smoothly into the community.

Booking Process:

- **Making Reservations:** Book your homestay well in advance, especially during peak tourist seasons. Please confirm all details, including the type of accommodation, activities included, and any dietary restrictions.
- **Confirming Details:** Please reconfirm your booking and any transportation arrangements a few days before your arrival. This ensures that everything is in place for a smooth arrival.

Village homestays and community tours in Thailand offer a rare opportunity to step off the beaten path and experience the country's rich cultural heritage intimately and authentically. Whether you're cooking alongside a local family, learning traditional crafts, or simply sharing stories around a fire, these experiences create lasting memories and meaningful connections. By choosing a homestay, you're gaining a deeper understanding of Thai culture and contributing to the sustainability and preservation of these communities. As you plan your stay, take the time to prepare thoughtfully, embrace the opportunity to learn and engage, and open yourself to the warmth and hospitality these villages offer.

CHAPTER 7: HIDDEN GEMS AND OFF-THE-BEATEN-PATH LOCATIONS

While Thailand's bustling cities and famous beaches often steal the spotlight, the country's less-traveled northern regions are a treasure trove of hidden gems waiting to be discovered. Northern Thailand is rich in culture, history, and natural beauty, offering a quieter, more intimate experience for those willing to venture off the beaten path. In this chapter, we'll guide you through Northern Thailand's best-kept secrets—from charming villages and stunning natural attractions to cultural landmarks and adventurous activities showcasing the region's unique charm.

Discovering Northern Thailand's Hidden Treasures

Northern Thailand is home to numerous quaint towns and villages that offer an authentic glimpse into traditional Thai life. These locations are perfect for travelers seeking peace, tranquility, and a deeper connection with the local culture.

CHAPTER 7: HIDDEN GEMS AND OFF-THE-BEATEN-PATH LOCATIONS

Mae Hong Son: Scenic Landscapes and Hill Tribe Cultures

- **Overview:** Tucked away in the mountainous border region near Myanmar, Mae Hong Son is a picturesque town surrounded by misty valleys and dense forests. It's known for its rich cultural tapestry, influenced by the Shan people and various hill tribes.
- **Highlights:** Visitors can explore traditional Shan temples, such as Wat Chong Kham and Wat Phra That Doi Kong Mu, or take a boat trip on the scenic Pai River. The town is also a gateway to hill tribe villages where you can learn about the customs and lifestyles of the Karen, Lahu, and Hmong people.

Chiang Dao: Limestone Caves and Majestic Mountains

- **Overview:** Located about 70 kilometers north of Chiang Mai, Chiang Dao is a small town nestled at the base of Doi Chiang Dao, Thailand's third-highest peak. The area is renowned for its dramatic limestone cliffs, verdant forests, and ancient caves.
- **Highlights:** The Chiang Dao Cave complex is a must-visit, with its network of caverns filled with stalactites, stalagmites, and Buddhist shrines. For adventure seekers, trekking to the summit of Doi Chiang Dao offers breathtaking views and a chance to experience the region's diverse flora and fauna.

Phayao: A Tranquil Lake and Local Markets

- **Overview:** Phayao is a peaceful town centered around Phayao Lake, one of Northern Thailand's largest freshwater lakes. The city is less frequented by tourists, making it an ideal spot for those seeking a serene escape.
- **Highlights:** Stroll along the lakeside promenade, visit Wat Tilok Aram (a submerged temple in the middle of the lake), or explore the local markets to sample regional specialties and buy handmade crafts.

Mae Salong: Chinese Tea Plantations and Historical Sites

- **Overview:** Mae Salong, also known as Santikhiri, is a mountain village with a unique history. Initially settled by Chinese Nationalist soldiers after World War II, the village is now famous for its tea plantations and stunning views of the surrounding hills.
- **Highlights:** Visit the tea plantations to learn about the tea-making process and taste locally grown oolong tea. The village is also home to the Martyr's Memorial Hall, which provides insight into Mae Salong's complex history. Don't miss the opportunity to trek through the surrounding hills dotted with small villages and vibrant markets.

Highlighting Unique Natural Attractions

Northern Thailand is full of natural beauty, from mist-covered mountains to lush agricultural valleys. Some lesser-known natural attractions offer stunning scenery and a

CHAPTER 7: HIDDEN GEMS AND OFF-THE-BEATEN-PATH LOCATIONS

peaceful retreat from the more touristy areas.

Phu Chi Fa: A Mountain Viewpoint with a Sea of Mist

- **Overview:** Phu Chi Fa is a mountain in the Phi Pan Nam Range near the Laos border. The mountain is famous for its spectacular viewpoint, which offers a breathtaking sea of mist at dawn, with the sun rising over the mountains and the Mekong River in the distance.
- **Highlights:** The best time to visit Phu Chi Fa is in the early morning to catch the sunrise. Afterward, you can explore the surrounding area, which is home to Hmong and Yao villages. The trek to the viewpoint is relatively easy, making it accessible to most travelers.

Doi Ang Khang: Royal Agricultural Station and Flower Gardens

- **Overview:** Doi Ang Khang is a mountain located near the Myanmar border, known for its cool climate and scenic beauty. The Royal Agricultural Station Ang Khang, established by King Bhumibol Adulyadej, is a key attraction focusing on sustainable agriculture and horticulture.
- **Highlights:** Visitors can explore the station's beautifully maintained flower gardens, orchards, and greenhouses, which showcase a variety of temperate plants and fruits not typically found in Thailand. The surrounding area is also great for bird watching, trekking, and visiting hill tribe villages.

Recommending Cultural and Historical Sites

Northern Thailand is steeped in history and culture, with many sites that offer a deep insight into the region's heritage. Here are a few must-visit cultural and historical landmarks.

Wat Phra That Lampang Luang: An Ancient Temple with Traditional Architecture

- **Overview:** Located in Lampang Province, Wat Phra That Lampang Luang is one of Northern Thailand's most revered temples. Dating back to the 13th century, the temple is an outstanding example of Lanna architecture, with its wooden structures and intricate carvings.
- **Highlights:** The temple's main chedi is said to contain a relic of the Buddha, making it a significant pilgrimage site. Visitors can also admire the temple's murals, among the oldest in Thailand, and explore the surrounding complex, including a museum and several other historic buildings.

CHAPTER 7: HIDDEN GEMS AND OFF-THE-BEATEN-PATH LOCATIONS

Wat Phra Kaew

Chiang Saen: Historical Ruins and Mekong River Views

- **Overview:** Chiang Saen is an ancient town located on the banks of the Mekong River, near the Golden Triangle, where Thailand, Laos, and Myanmar meet. Once the capital of the Lanna Kingdom, a town is now a quiet place with a rich historical legacy.
- **Highlights:** Explore the ruins of ancient temples, such as Wat Pa Sak and Wat Phra That Chedi Luang, which date back to the 13th century. The town's location along the Mekong River also offers stunning views and a peaceful atmosphere, perfect for relaxing after a day of sightseeing.

Detailing Adventure Activities in the Region

For outdoor enthusiasts, Northern Thailand offers a wide range of adventure activities that allow you to explore the region's natural beauty up close. Here are some top recommendations.

Trekking in Pai: Waterfalls and Hot Springs

- **Overview:** Pai is a small town in Mae Hong Son Province that has become a popular destination for trekkers and nature lovers. The surrounding area has waterfalls, hot springs, and lush forests, making it ideal for outdoor activities.
- **Highlights:** Join a guided trek to explore the nearby Mae Yen Waterfall, visit the Pai Hot Springs for a relaxing soak, or hike through the Pai Canyon for stunning views of the valley. The area is also home to several hill tribe villages, where you can learn about local culture and traditions.

Cycling in Nan: Scenic Routes and Rural Landscapes

- **Overview:** Nan is a lesser-known province in Northern Thailand that offers some of the best cycling routes in the country. The province is characterized by rolling hills, lush valleys, and traditional villages, making it a cyclist paradise.
- **Highlights:** Rent a bike and explore the scenic routes around Nan, such as the winding roads through the Doi Phu Kha National Park or the peaceful trails along the Nan River. Along the way, you'll pass through small

villages where you can stop for a meal and interact with the friendly locals.

Bamboo Rafting in Mae Taeng: River Adventures with Local Guides

- **Overview:** Mae Taeng, located just north of Chiang Mai, is known for its picturesque river and outdoor adventure opportunities. Bamboo rafting is a popular activity that allows you to float down the river and take in the natural beauty of the surrounding forests and mountains.
- **Highlights:** Join a bamboo rafting tour led by local guides. The guides will navigate you through the gentle rapids and calm stretches of the Mae Taeng River. The experience is both relaxing and exhilarating, offering a unique way to connect with the natural environment.

Northern Thailand's hidden gems offer a world of discovery for those willing to explore beyond the usual tourist routes. Whether you're wandering through ancient temples, trekking to remote hill tribe villages, or simply enjoying the tranquility of a mountain lake, these off-the-beaten-path locations provide a more profound, more authentic experience of Thailand's rich cultural and natural heritage. By venturing into these lesser-known areas, you'll gain a greater appreciation for the country's diversity and create memories that will last a lifetime. As you plan your journey, consider adding some of these hidden treasures to your itinerary—you won't be disappointed.

Secret Beaches and Islands in Southern Thailand

Southern Thailand is famous for its stunning beaches and idyllic islands, drawing visitors worldwide. However, while popular destinations like Phuket, Koh Phi Phi, and Koh Samui often take center stage, the region also boasts numerous lesser-known gems that offer breathtaking scenery and a serene escape from the crowds. In this section, we'll explore some of Southern Thailand's best-kept secrets—from pristine islands and secluded beaches to unique marine activities—all while emphasizing the importance of sustainable travel to preserve these natural wonders.

Discovering Lesser-Known Islands

For those seeking a more tranquil and authentic island experience, Southern Thailand offers several hidden paradises to escape the tourist crowds and immerse yourself in nature.

Koh Lipe: Pristine Beaches and Crystal-Clear Waters

- **Overview:** Often referred to as the "Maldives of Thailand," Koh Lipe is a small island located in the Andaman Sea, near the border with Malaysia. Despite its growing popularity, Koh Lipe remains less crowded than many other Thai islands, offering visitors a slice of paradise with its powdery white sand beaches and turquoise waters.
- **Highlights:** The island's three main beaches—Pattaya Beach, Sunrise Beach, and Sunset Beach—each offer something unique, from vibrant nightlife to peaceful sunrises. Koh Lipe is also part of the Tarutao National Marine Park, making it a great base for exploring nearby

uninhabited islands and coral reefs.

Sea Ko Lipe

Koh Kradan: Coral Reefs and Marine Life

- **Overview:** Koh Kradan is a small, picturesque island in the Trang Archipelago, known for its stunning coral reefs and vibrant marine life. The island is largely undeveloped, with only a few low-key resorts and plenty of untouched natural beauty.
- **Highlights:** The main attraction here is snorkeling—just a short swim from the beach, you'll find colorful coral gardens teeming with fish. The island's calm, shallow waters are perfect for beginners, while more experienced snorkelers can explore the reefs further offshore. Koh Kradan's peaceful atmosphere and lack of commercialization make it an ideal retreat for those looking to disconnect and unwind.

Koh Yao Noi: Peaceful Atmosphere and Local Fishing Villages

- **Overview:** Situated between Phuket and Krabi, Koh Yao Noi is a tranquil island that offers a glimpse into traditional Thai life. Unlike its more developed neighbors, Koh Yao Noi has retained its rural charm, with small fishing villages, rice paddies, and rubber plantations dotting the landscape.
- **Highlights:** The island is perfect for those who want to experience Southern Thailand's natural beauty without the crowds. Activities on Koh Yao Noi include cycling through the countryside, kayaking around the island's coastline, and visiting local markets. The island's laid-back vibe and friendly locals make it a wonderful place

to relax and immerse yourself in the local culture.

Recommending Secluded Beaches

If you're dreaming of a quiet beach where you can relax and soak up the sun without the hustle and bustle of tourist crowds, Southern Thailand has plenty of hidden spots waiting to be discovered.

Ao Leuk Bay (Koh Tao): Snorkeling and Tranquility

- **Overview:** Ao Leuk Bay is a hidden gem on the eastern coast of Koh Tao, an island known for its diving spots. The bay is one of the most beautiful and tranquil on the island, with crystal-clear waters, soft sand, and a peaceful atmosphere.
- **Highlights:** Ao Leuk is an excellent spot for snorkeling, with vibrant coral reefs just a short swim from the shore. The bay's calm waters make it a great place for beginners, and the abundance of marine life, including colorful fish and sea turtles, adds to the experience. The beach is less crowded than other parts of Koh Tao, offering a serene escape for those looking to relax and enjoy the natural surroundings.

Freedom Beach (Phuket): White Sand and Clear Water

- **Overview:** Located on Phuket's west coast, Freedom Beach is one of the island's most secluded and picturesque beaches. Accessible only by boat or via a steep jungle path, this hidden beach is a true tropical paradise with its white sand and clear blue waters.

- **Highlights:** Freedom Beach offers a more peaceful alternative to Phuket's busier beaches, making it perfect for sunbathing, swimming, or simply enjoying the tranquility. The beach is surrounded by lush greenery and granite rocks, providing a stunning backdrop for your day in the sun. Due to its remote location, Freedom Beach remains relatively quiet, even during peak season.

Kantiang Bay (Koh Lanta): Secluded and Scenic Views

- **Overview:** Kantiang Bay is a beautiful, crescent-shaped beach located on the southern tip of Koh Lanta. Known for its soft sand, clear waters, and scenic views, Kantiang Bay is a haven for those seeking solitude and natural beauty.
- **Highlights:** The bay is perfect for swimming, snorkeling, or simply relaxing on the sand with a good book. The surrounding hills provide a dramatic backdrop, and the beach's remote location means it's often quiet, even during the high season. There are a few beachfront restaurants and bars where you can enjoy a meal or a drink while enjoying the stunning sunset.

Detailing Unique Marine Activities

Southern Thailand is a playground for water sports enthusiasts, offering a variety of activities that allow you to explore its underwater world and stunning coastal landscapes.

CHAPTER 7: HIDDEN GEMS AND OFF-THE-BEATEN-PATH LOCATIONS

Diving in the Similan Islands: Vibrant Coral Reefs and Diverse Marine Life

- **Overview:** The Similan Islands, located off the coast of Phang Nga Province, are considered one of the best diving destinations in the world. The islands are part of a national park and are renowned for their crystal-clear waters, vibrant coral reefs, and diverse marine life.
- **Highlights:** Divers can explore various dive sites, each offering something different—from colorful coral gardens to dramatic underwater rock formations and deep blue waters teeming with fish. The Similan Islands are home to many marine life, including manta rays, whale sharks, and turtles. Whether you're a seasoned diver or a beginner, the Similan Islands offer an unforgettable diving experience.

Similan Islands

Kayaking in Ao Thalane: Mangroves and Karst Formations

- **Overview:** Ao Thalane, located near Krabi, is a stunning area known for its mangrove forests and towering karst formations. The best way to explore this natural wonder is by kayak, allowing you to navigate through narrow channels and get up close to the diverse wildlife.
- **Highlights:** As you paddle through the calm waters, you'll see a variety of birds, monkeys, and other wildlife that call the mangroves home. The towering limestone cliffs and hidden lagoons create a surreal landscape best appreciated by the water. Kayaking tours are available

for all skill levels, making this a perfect activity for nature lovers and adventure seekers alike.

Snorkeling in Koh Rok: Clear Waters and Abundant Fish

- **Overview:** Koh Rok is a pair of islands in the Andaman Sea known for their stunning beaches and excellent snorkeling spots. The islands are part of the Mu Koh Lanta National Park, which ensures that the marine environment remains pristine and protected.
- **Highlights:** The waters around Koh Rok are incredibly clear, making it easy to spot various marine life, including colorful fish, rays, and even small sharks. The coral reefs here are some of the healthiest in the region, providing a vibrant underwater landscape for snorkelers to explore. The islands themselves are uninhabited, adding to the sense of seclusion and tranquility.

Providing Tips for Sustainable Travel

As you explore these hidden gems, it's important to do so responsibly to ensure that these beautiful places remain unspoiled for future generations. Here are some tips for sustainable travel in Southern Thailand.

Eco-Friendly Accommodations:

- **Green Hotels and Sustainable Resorts:** Look for accommodations that prioritize sustainability, such as those that use renewable energy, reduce water consumption, and support local communities. Many Eco-friendly resorts in Southern Thailand are committed to preserving the environment while providing a comfortable and memorable stay.

Responsible Snorkeling:

- **Coral-Safe Sunscreen:** When snorkeling or diving, use reef-safe sunscreen to protect coral reefs from harmful chemicals. These sunscreens are free from oxybenzone and octinoxate, which can cause coral bleaching.
- **No-Touch Policies:** While touching coral or marine life is tempting, resisting the urge is essential. Touching can damage delicate ecosystems, so enjoy the underwater beauty with your eyes and leave everything as you found it.

Supporting Local Businesses:

- **Eating at Local Restaurants:** Choose meals at locally-owned restaurants rather than international chains. This supports the local economy and allows you to try authentic Thai cuisine.
- **Buying from Local Artisans:** Purchase souvenirs and crafts from local artisans rather than mass-produced items. This helps preserve traditional crafts and supports the livelihoods of local communities.

Southern Thailand's secret beaches and islands offer a natural beauty and tranquility sanctuary, far from the crowded tourist hot spots. Whether you're diving in the crystal-clear waters of the Similan Islands, relaxing on the secluded sands of

CHAPTER 7: HIDDEN GEMS AND OFF-THE-BEATEN-PATH LOCATIONS

Kantiang Bay, or exploring the mangrove forests of Ao Thalane by kayak, these hidden gems provide an unforgettable experience for those willing to venture off the beaten path. By traveling sustainably and responsibly, you can help preserve these pristine environments, ensuring that they remain just as beautiful for future travelers to discover. So pack your bags, leave the crowds behind, and set out to explore the serene side of Southern Thailand.

Offbeat Adventures in Eastern Thailand

Eastern Thailand is a region often overlooked by tourists in favor of more well-trodden destinations. However, this area is brimming with hidden treasures, offering diverse experiences that cater to adventurers and culture enthusiasts alike. From tranquil provinces and stunning natural parks to rich cultural sites and thrilling outdoor activities, Eastern Thailand is the perfect destination for those looking to explore the road less traveled. In this section, we'll guide you through the lesser-known provinces, unique natural attractions, cultural landmarks, and adventure activities that make Eastern Thailand a must-visit for any intrepid traveler.

Exploring Lesser-Known Provinces

Eastern Thailand is home to several provinces that mainstream tourists often skip, yet these areas offer unique experiences and a glimpse into Thailand's quieter, more authentic side.

Trat: Gateway to Koh Chang and Quiet Beaches

- **Overview:** Trat is a small province near the Cambodian border. It serves as the gateway to the stunning islands of Koh Chang, Koh Mak, and Koh Kood. While these islands are well-known, the province of Trat itself remains peaceful and largely untouched by mass tourism.
- **Highlights:** Explore Trat's quiet beaches, such as those found on Laem Ngop and Ban Chuen, where you can relax without the crowds. The town of Trat is charming, with its traditional wooden houses, bustling night markets, and historical temples like Wat Buppharam. You can also easily access the nearby islands from Trat for further exploration.

Chanthaburi: Gem Markets and Historical Sites

- **Overview:** Chanthaburi is a province famous for its gem markets and rich history. The town is known as the "City of the Moon" and has a vibrant mix of cultures reflected in its architecture and local traditions.
- **Highlights:** Visit the Chanthaboon Waterfront Community to admire the colonial architecture and shop for local crafts. The Chanthaburi Gem Market is a must-see, where traders worldwide come to buy and sell precious stones. The province also has several beautiful churches, such as the Cathedral of the Immaculate Conception, and historic sites like the Taksin Maharat Shrine.

CHAPTER 7: HIDDEN GEMS AND OFF-THE-BEATEN-PATH LOCATIONS

Sa Kaeo: Natural Parks and Border Markets

- **Overview:** Sa Kaeo is a province located along the border with Cambodia. It is known for its natural parks and vibrant border markets. Nature and culture intertwine here, offering a variety of experiences for adventurous travelers.
- **Highlights:** Explore the natural beauty of Sa Kaeo in Pang Sida National Park, where you can see waterfalls, wildlife, and scenic viewpoints. The province is also home to the Aranyaprathet Border Market, one of Thailand's largest and most diverse markets, where you can find everything from clothing and electronics to traditional crafts and local foods.

Highlighting Unique Natural Attractions

Eastern Thailand boasts a variety of natural wonders that offer breathtaking scenery and a host of outdoor activities. Here are some must-visit natural attractions in the region.

Khao Khitchakut National Park: Pilgrimage Trails and Mountaintop Views

- **Overview:** Khao Khitchakut National Park is a place of spiritual significance and natural beauty in Chanthaburi Province. The park is famous for its pilgrimage trail, which leads to a mountaintop shrine that attracts thousands of worshipers each year.
- **Highlights:** The pilgrimage to the summit of Khao Phra Bat takes you through lush forests and up steep trails,

rewarding you with panoramic views of the surrounding countryside. At the top, you'll find a revered footprint of the Buddha, along with a serene atmosphere perfect for reflection. The park is also home to waterfalls and rich biodiversity, making it an excellent destination for nature lovers.

Namtok Phlio National Park: Waterfalls and Historical Memorials

- **Overview:** Namtok Phlio National Park, also located in Chanthaburi Province, is known for its stunning waterfalls and historical significance. The park is famous for locals and tourists who want to enjoy the area's natural beauty.
- **Highlights:** The park's centerpiece is Phlio Waterfall, a majestic cascade surrounded by lush greenery. The pool at the waterfall's base is filled with large fish, making it a popular spot for feeding and swimming. The park also features historical memorials, including the Phra Nang Ruea Lom Stupa, which commemorates a royal consort of King Rama V.

Recommending Cultural and Historical Sites

Eastern Thailand is rich in cultural heritage, with several sites offering deep insights into the region's history and traditions. Here are a few cultural landmarks worth visiting.

CHAPTER 7: HIDDEN GEMS AND OFF-THE-BEATEN-PATH LOCATIONS

Chanthaboon Waterfront Community: Colonial Architecture and Local Crafts

- **Overview:** The Chanthaboon Waterfront Community in Chanthaburi Town is a historic area that showcases the province's colonial past. The community is situated along the Chanthaburi River, where traders from France, China, and other countries once conducted business.
- **Highlights:** Stroll along the narrow streets lined with well-preserved colonial-era buildings, many of which have been converted into cafes, galleries, and boutique shops. Local artisans sell handmade crafts, traditional foods, and souvenirs, providing a perfect opportunity to support local businesses and take home a piece of Chanthaburi's culture.

Ancient City of Mueang Boran: Historical Replicas and Cultural Exhibits

- **Overview:** Also known as the "Ancient City," Mueang Boran is an open-air museum located near Bangkok that features replicas of Thailand's most important historical and cultural landmarks. While not technically in Eastern Thailand, it's easily accessible and provides a comprehensive overview of the country's heritage.
- **Highlights:** The site covers over 200 acres and includes replicas of famous temples, palaces, and monuments from across Thailand. It's a great place to learn about the region's history and culture in a single day, with exhibits that include traditional Thai houses, market scenes, and religious icons.

Detailing Adventure Activities in the Region

Eastern Thailand offers adventure seekers a wide range of outdoor activities, from trekking through dense forests to cycling along scenic coastal roads. Here are some top recommendations for adventurous travelers.

Trekking in Khao Soi Dao: Forest Trails and Wildlife Spotting

- **Overview:** Khao Soi Dao, located in Chanthaburi Province, is a mountain that offers some of the best trekking opportunities in Eastern Thailand. The area is known for its diverse flora and fauna and its challenging trails that lead through dense forests and up to high-altitude viewpoints.
- **Highlights:** The trek to the summit of Khao Soi Dao is a rewarding experience. You can see rare wildlife such as hornbills, gibbons, and even wild elephants. The trail passes through several waterfalls and lush landscapes, making it a scenic and exhilarating journey. For those who prefer a shorter trek, more accessible trails offer beautiful views without the demanding climb.

Cycling in Koh Mak: Quiet Roads and Scenic Views

- **Overview:** Koh Mak is a small, idyllic island in Trat Province known for its quiet roads and stunning coastal scenery. The island's flat terrain and limited traffic make it ideal for cycling enthusiasts looking to explore at a leisurely pace.

CHAPTER 7: HIDDEN GEMS AND OFF-THE-BEATEN-PATH LOCATIONS

- **Highlights:** Rent a bike and cycle around the island, stopping at secluded beaches, coconut plantations, and small fishing villages along the way. The island's relaxed atmosphere and breathtaking views make it a perfect spot for a day of exploration. Be sure to visit Ao Kao Beach and Ao Suan Yai Beach, two of the island's most beautiful stretches of sand.

Exploring Thap Lan National Park: Hiking, Camping, and Rare Flora

- **Overview:** Thap Lan National Park, straddling the border of Nakhon Ratchasima and Prachinburi provinces, is one of Thailand's largest national parks and a UNESCO World Heritage Site. The park is known for its diverse ecosystems, including dense forests, rolling hills, and rare flora, such as giant Dipterocarp trees.
- **Highlights:** Thap Lan is a paradise for hikers and nature lovers, with numerous trails that lead through the park's varied landscapes. The park offers opportunities for wildlife spotting, bird watching, and discovering rare plant species. Camping is also popular, with several designated sites offering a chance to sleep under the stars in a pristine natural setting.

Eastern Thailand is a region rich in natural beauty, cultural heritage, and adventurous opportunities, making it an ideal destination for those looking to explore beyond the typical tourist hot spots. Whether you're trekking through the forests of Khao Soi Dao, cycling along the quiet roads of Koh Mak, or discovering the historical treasures of Chanthaburi, this part of Thailand offers a wealth of unique and unforgettable experiences. As you plan your journey, consider adding these offbeat adventures to your itinerary—you'll be rewarded with discovering a side of Thailand that few tourists can see.

CHAPTER 8: CULTURAL ETIQUETTE AND RESPECT

Thailand is known as the "Land of Smiles," reflecting its warm and welcoming culture. However, like any country, Thailand has its own set of cultural norms and etiquette that are important to understand and respect. By being mindful of these practices, you can ensure that your interactions with locals are positive and that you appropriately respect Thai traditions and customs. In this chapter, we'll explore the critical aspects of Thai etiquette, including the proper use of the 'Wai' greeting, how to behave in public places, the importance of respecting the monarchy, and general social etiquette rules.

The Dos and Don'ts of Thai Etiquette

Understanding and respecting Thai etiquette is essential for any visitor. Following these guidelines will demonstrate cultural sensitivity and foster positive interactions during your stay in Thailand.

The Importance of the 'Wai' Greeting

The 'Wai' is a traditional Thai greeting and a significant gesture of respect in Thai culture. It involves pressing your palms together prayerfully and bowing your head slightly. The Wai is a greeting and a way to say thank you, apologize, or show respect in various situations.

How to Wai:

- **Position of Hands:** Place your palms together with fingers pointing upwards, near your chest or face, depending on the level of respect you wish to show. The higher your hands, the more respect you are conveying. For most situations, a Wai with hands at chest level is appropriate.
- **Bowing the Head:** Accompany the Wai with a slight head bow. The depth of the bow can vary, but generally, a modest nod is sufficient in casual interactions.

When to Wai:

- **Greeting Elders:** Wai customarily greets elders as a sign of respect. This includes older relatives, teachers, and senior colleagues.
- **Saying Thank You:** The Wai is often used to express gratitude, especially after receiving a favor or gift.
- **Religious Settings:** When visiting temples or interacting with monks, a Wai is a respectful way to greet and show reverence.

Situations to Avoid:

- **Not Wai-ing to Children or Service Staff:** While Wai is important when greeting elders and superiors, it's not expected to Wai to those younger than you or service staff. Instead, a polite nod or smile is appropriate.
- **In Professional Settings:** A handshake is often more appropriate in business settings, particularly when interacting with non-Thai professionals. However, if a Thai person initiates a Wai, returning the gesture is polite.

Proper Behavior in Public Places

Respectful behavior in public places is highly valued in Thai culture. By following these guidelines, you can ensure that you behave appropriately and avoid any unintentional offense.

Dress Modestly:

- **Avoid Revealing Clothing:** In Thailand, dressing modestly is a sign of respect, especially when visiting temples, religious sites, or rural areas. It's important to cover your shoulders and knees. While beachwear is acceptable on the beach, it's considered inappropriate to wear it in public places outside of beach areas.

Public Displays of Affection:

- **Keeping it Minimal:** Public displays of affection, such as kissing or hugging, are generally frowned upon in Thai culture. It's best to keep such gestures private, as excessive affection in public can be seen as disrespectful.

Removing Shoes:

- **Entering Homes and Businesses:** It's customary to remove your shoes before entering someone's home, temples, and certain businesses like traditional massage shops. Look for signs or follow the locals' lead. Wearing clean, modest socks is also appreciated in places where shoes are removed.

Showing Respect to the Monarchy

The Thai royal family is deeply revered, and it's crucial to show respect towards the monarchy in all situations. Criticism or disrespect towards the monarchy is culturally insensitive and illegal under Thai law.

Standing for the Royal Anthem:

- **In Cinemas and Public Events:** The royal anthem is played before movies in cinemas and at some public events. It's essential to stand up as a sign of respect during the anthem, which honors the king.

Avoiding Criticism:

- **Of the Monarchy and Royal Family:** Criticism of the monarchy, even in casual conversation or on social media, is strictly prohibited and can result in severe legal consequences. It's best to avoid discussing the royal family altogether.

Respecting Royal Images:

- **Handling with Care:** Images of the king and the royal family are prominently displayed throughout Thailand in public places, businesses, and homes. Handling any image of the monarchy with care and respect is essential. Never step on or over any image of the king or royal family members, as this is considered extremely disrespectful.

General Social Etiquette Rules

Thai culture values harmony and respect in social interactions. Here are some general etiquette rules to follow during your stay.

Respecting Elders:

- **Giving Way:** When walking, it is polite to give way to elders, allowing them to pass first. This is especially important in crowded places.
- **Offering Seats:** On public transportation, always offer your seat to elders, monks, pregnant women, and those with young children.

Avoiding Confrontations:

- **Staying Calm and Smiling:** Thais generally avoid confrontations and value maintaining a calm and friendly demeanor. If you disagree, staying relaxed, avoiding raising your voice, and resolving the situation with a smile is essential. This approach is "saving face" and is critical to respectful interactions.

Using the Right Hand:

- **For Giving and Receiving Items:** When giving or receiving items, especially when offering food, gifts, or money, it's customary to use your right hand or both hands together. The left hand is considered less clean and should not be used for these actions.

Touching the Head:

- **Avoiding This Gesture:** In Thai culture, the head is considered the most sacred part of the body, and it's inappropriate to touch someone's head, even in a friendly manner. This is especially important with children, as touching their heads is seen as disrespectful.

Understanding and respecting Thai cultural etiquette is essential for ensuring positive and harmonious interactions during your visit. By following these guidelines—performing the Wai correctly, dressing modestly, or respecting the monarchy—you can navigate social situations confidently and gracefully. Thailand's rich cultural traditions are one of the many reasons why it's such a beloved destination, and by showing respect for these customs, you'll not only enrich your travel experience but also earn the respect and warmth of the Thai people you meet along the way.

CHAPTER 8: CULTURAL ETIQUETTE AND RESPECT

Visiting Temples and Sacred Sites

Thailand is a country deeply rooted in Buddhism, and its temples (known as wats) and sacred sites are among the most important cultural and spiritual landmarks. These places are stunning architectural wonders and active centers of worship, making it essential for visitors to approach them with respect and understanding. In this section, we'll guide you on how to dress appropriately, behave respectfully, and engage with monks during your visits to temples and sacred sites. We'll also highlight some of the most significant temples in Thailand that you should not miss on your journey.

Dress Code for Temple Visits

When visiting temples in Thailand, it's important to dress modestly as a sign of respect for the sacred nature of these sites. Here are specific guidelines to follow:

Covering Shoulders and Knees:

- **No Shorts or Sleeveless Tops:** Both men and women are expected to cover their shoulders and knees when entering temple grounds. This means wearing long pants, skirts, or dresses that extend below the knees and tops that cover the shoulders. Avoid sleeveless shirts, tank tops, and shorts.
- **Sarongs and Shawls:** If you're caught unprepared, many temples offer sarongs or shawls for a small fee or donation that you can use to cover up before entering.

Removing Hats and Shoes:

- **Before Entering Temple Buildings:** It is customary to remove your shoes before entering any temple building. This applies to the main hall (*ubosot*), where the principal Buddha image is kept, and other sacred structures within the temple complex. Hats should also be removed as a sign of respect.

Avoiding Bright Colors:

- **Opting for Neutral, Respectful Attire:** While there is no strict rule against bright colors, wearing neutral or muted tones is generally more respectful when visiting temples. This helps maintain the serene atmosphere of the site and ensures that your attire does not distract from the spiritual environment.

Proper Conduct Within Temple Grounds

Respectful behavior is essential when visiting temples in Thailand. These guidelines will help you navigate the expected conduct within temple grounds:

Silent Reverence:

- **Keeping Noise to a Minimum:** Temples are places of worship and meditation, so it's important to keep noise levels low. Speak softly, avoid loud conversations, and refrain from using your phone or playing music while on temple grounds.

CHAPTER 8: CULTURAL ETIQUETTE AND RESPECT

Not Pointing Feet:

- **Avoiding Pointing Feet Towards Buddha Images:** In Thai culture, the feet are considered the lowest and dirtiest part of the body, and pointing your feet at someone, especially at a Buddha image, is considered highly disrespectful. When sitting in front of a Buddha image, sit with your legs folded to the side or cross-legged, ensuring your feet are not pointing directly at the image.

Sitting Etiquette:

- **Sitting with Legs to the Side:** When sitting on the floor in a temple, avoid stretching your legs out in front of you. Instead, sit with your legs folded to one side or cross-legged. This shows humility and respect in the presence of sacred objects.

Photography Rules:

- **Asking Permission and Respecting Signs:** While photography is generally allowed in many temples, it's important to ask permission before taking photos, especially if monks or worshipers are present. Some temples may have signs indicating areas where photography is prohibited, particularly inside the main hall or near Buddha images. Always respect these signs to avoid offending.

Interacting with Monks

Monks hold a revered position in Thai society, and their interactions should be conducted with the utmost respect. Here's how to engage respectfully with monks:

Thai Buddhist Monks

Avoiding Physical Contact:

- **Especially for Women:** In Thai Buddhist tradition, monks are not allowed to touch or be touched by women. Women should avoid handing anything directly to a monk; instead, place the item on a cloth or in a neutral area where the monk can pick it up without contact. Men should also maintain a respectful distance and avoid unnecessary physical contact.

Offering Alms:

- **Respectful Presentation and Early Morning Rituals:** Offering alms to monks is common in Thailand and is typically done in the early morning. If you wish to participate, prepare offerings such as food, drinks, or flowers and present them respectfully, usually kneeling with a bowed head. The monk will then give a blessing in return. Remember to avoid offering meat or any items that are forbidden in the monk's dietary restrictions.

Addressing Monks:

- **Using Polite Language and the Wai Gesture:** Use polite and formal language when speaking to monks. Greeting monks with a Wai (the traditional Thai gesture of respect) is also customary. You place your hands together in a prayer-like position and bow your head slightly. Monks may not always return the Wai, as they are considered higher in social status.

Significant Temples to Visit

Thailand is home to thousands of temples, each with its own unique history and significance. Here are some of the most important temples that you should consider visiting during your travels:

Wat Phra Kaew: The Emerald Buddha Temple, Bangkok

- **Overview:** Wat Phra Kaew, located within the grounds of the Grand Palace in Bangkok, is one of Thailand's most sacred temples. It houses the Emerald Buddha, a highly revered image carved from a single block of jade.
- **Highlights:** The temple complex features intricate murals, golden stupas, and ornate buildings. The Emerald Buddha, though small in size, symbolizes Thailand's sovereignty and is deeply venerated by the Thai people. Note that photography is not allowed inside the main chapel.

CHAPTER 8: CULTURAL ETIQUETTE AND RESPECT

Wat Phra Sri Temple, Thailand

Wat Pho: The Reclining Buddha, Bangkok

- **Overview:** Wat Pho, also known as the Temple of the Reclining Buddha, is one of Bangkok's oldest and largest temples. It is famous for its massive reclining Buddha statue, which measures 46 meters long and is covered in gold leaf.
- **Highlights:** Besides the reclining Buddha, Wat Pho is home to over a thousand Buddha images and an extensive collection of murals depicting various aspects of Thai culture and history. The temple is also the birthplace of traditional Thai massage, and visitors can receive a massage at the on-site school.

Wat Arun: The Temple of Dawn, Bangkok

- **Overview:** Wat Arun, or the Temple of Dawn, is one of Bangkok's most iconic landmarks, located on the banks of the Chao Phraya River. The temple's towering spires, known as *prangs*, are decorated with colorful porcelain and seashells, creating a dazzling effect when illuminated by the sun.
- **Highlights:** Climbing to the top of the central prang offers stunning panoramic views of the river and the city. Wat Arun is lovely when the temple is bathed in a golden glow at sunset. The temple's unique architecture and riverside location make it a must-visit site in Bangkok.

CHAPTER 8: CULTURAL ETIQUETTE AND RESPECT

Wat Phra That Doi Suthep: Hilltop Temple, Chiang Mai

- **Overview:** Wat Phra That Doi Suthep is a revered temple on Doi Suthep mountain, overlooking Chiang Mai. It is an important pilgrimage site and offers breathtaking views of the surrounding area.
- **Highlights:** The temple's golden chedi, which enshrines a relic of the Buddha, is the focal point of the complex. Visitors can reach the temple by climbing a staircase of 306 steps flanked by elaborately decorated *naga* (serpent) statues. Once at the top, you can explore the temple grounds, admire the intricate Lanna architecture, and take in the panoramic views of Chiang Mai and the valley below.

Visiting temples and sacred sites in Thailand is a deeply enriching experience that offers insight into the country's spiritual and cultural heritage. By dressing appropriately, acting respectfully, and following the guidelines provided in this chapter, you can ensure that your visits to these holy places are both respectful and meaningful. Whether you're marveling at the Emerald Buddha in Bangkok, exploring the hilltop temple of Doi Suthep, or simply soaking in the serene atmosphere of a local wat, these experiences will undoubtedly leave a lasting impression on your journey through Thailand.

Engaging Respectfully with Locals

One of the most rewarding aspects of traveling in Thailand is the opportunity to engage with the local people, who are known for their warmth and hospitality. However, understanding the nuances of Thai social etiquette is crucial to ensuring that these interactions are positive and respectful. In this section, we'll explore how to enhance your communication with locals by learning basic Thai phrases, navigating social interactions, understanding the importance of personal space and body language, and participating respectfully in local customs and traditions.

The Importance of Learning Basic Thai Phrases

While many Thais in tourist areas speak some English, learning a few basic Thai phrases can greatly enhance your interactions with locals. Even a small effort to speak the language is often met with appreciation and can help you connect more deeply with the people you meet.

Common Greetings:

- **"Sawasdee" (Hello/Goodbye):** The most common greeting in Thailand, "Sawasdee," is used for both hello and goodbye. It's often accompanied by a slight bow with hands pressed together in a prayer-like gesture, known as the *Wai*.
- **"Khob Khun" (Thank you):** Expressing gratitude is important in Thai culture. "Khob Khun" is the standard way to say thank you, and adding "kha" for women or "rub" for men at the end of the phrase makes it even more polite.

Polite Expressions:

- **"Kha" for Women, "Krub" for Men:** In Thai, adding "kha" (for women) or "krub" (for men) at the end of a sentence makes the phrase polite and respectful. For example, "Sawasdee kha" (for women) or "Sawasdee krub" (for men) is a polite way to greet someone.
- **"Mai pen rai" (No worries/It's okay):** This phrase reflects the laid-back attitude of Thai culture. It's used to downplay a mistake or inconvenience or as a response to an apology, similar to saying "no problem" in English.

Asking for Help:

- **"Khun pood pasa ang-grit dai mai?" (Do you speak English?):** This phrase is useful when you need assistance but need clarification on whether the person speaks English. It's polite and shows that you're trying to communicate in their language.

Navigating Social Interactions

Understanding how to engage in social interactions respectfully is key to building positive relationships with locals. Here are some guidelines to help you navigate these encounters.

Making Eye Contact:

- **Appropriate Levels:** In Thai culture, direct eye contact can be seen as aggressive or confrontational, especially in more formal situations. It's best to maintain gentle eye contact, particularly when interacting with elders or those in positions of authority.

Personal Space:

- **Respecting Boundaries:** Thais generally value personal space, especially with strangers. While friendly and hospitable, physical closeness is usually reserved for close friends and family. Avoid standing too close or touching people you've just met.

Conversation Topics:

- **Avoiding Sensitive Subjects:** While Thais are generally open and friendly, specific topics such as politics, the monarchy, and religion can be sensitive. It's best to steer clear of these subjects in casual conversation. Instead, focus on lighthearted topics like food, travel, or Thai culture.

The Significance of Personal Space and Body Language

Non-verbal communication plays a significant role in Thai culture. Awareness of the local body language and personal space norms can help you avoid unintentional offenses.

Gestures to Avoid:

- **Pointing and Beckoning with Fingers:** Pointing at people or objects is considered rude in Thailand. If you need to indicate something, it's better to gesture with

CHAPTER 8: CULTURAL ETIQUETTE AND RESPECT

your whole hand. Similarly, beckoning someone with your fingers is impolite; instead, use your hand with the palm facing down to signal someone to come over.

Handing Objects:

- **Using Both Hands or the Right Hand:** When giving or receiving something, especially to or from someone older or of higher status, it's respectful to use both hands. If that's not practical, using your right hand while lightly touching your left hand to your right elbow is also considered polite.

Smiling:

- **As a Form of Communication:** Thailand is known as the "Land of Smiles," and smiling is an important aspect of nonverbal communication. Smiles express a range of emotions, from happiness and friendliness to politeness and even to diffuse awkward situations. A genuine smile can go a long way in showing respect and building rapport.

Participating in Local Customs and Traditions

Engaging with local customs and traditions is a wonderful way to immerse yourself in Thai culture. However, it's essential to do so with respect and understanding.

Taking Part in Festivals:

- **Following Local Customs and Dress Code:** Thailand hosts numerous festivals throughout the year, such as Songkran (Thai New Year) and Loy Krathong (Festival of Lights). When participating, it's important to follow local customs, such as dressing modestly and behaving respectfully, especially during religious ceremonies.

Visiting Local Homes:

- **Bringing Gifts and Removing Shoes:** If you're invited to a local's home, it is customary to receive a small gift, such as fruit or sweets. Upon entering the home, always remove your shoes at the door as a sign of respect. It's also polite to avoid stepping on the threshold, as it is believed to be home to protective spirits.

Supporting Local Businesses:

- **Shopping at Markets and Hiring Local Guides:** One of the best ways to engage with the community is by supporting local businesses. Shopping at local markets provides an authentic experience and helps sustain the local economy. When exploring natural or cultural sites, consider hiring local guides who can offer valuable insights and ensure your visit respects the area's traditions and environment.

Engaging respectfully with locals is an essential part of traveling in Thailand. You can ensure that your interactions

CHAPTER 8: CULTURAL ETIQUETTE AND RESPECT

are positive and meaningful by learning basic Thai phrases, understanding social norms, respecting personal space and body language, and participating thoughtfully in local customs. The warmth and hospitality of the Thai people are among the country's greatest treasures, and by approaching each interaction with respect and openness, you'll enrich your travel experience and create lasting connections with the people you meet along the way.

CHAPTER 9: SAFETY TIPS FOR SOLO TRAVELERS

Traveling solo can be an enriching experience, offering a sense of freedom and personal discovery. However, it also comes with unique challenges and risks, especially when navigating unfamiliar urban environments. By staying vigilant and taking precautions, solo travelers can enjoy their journeys while minimizing potential dangers. In this chapter, we'll cover essential safety tips for solo travelers, including how to stay safe in urban areas, use public transport securely, choose safe accommodations, and enjoy nightlife without compromising safety.

Staying Safe in Urban Areas

While urban areas in Thailand are generally safe, they can present certain risks, particularly for solo travelers. Being aware of your surroundings and taking proactive steps to protect yourself is crucial for a secure and enjoyable trip.

Situational Awareness:

- **Avoiding Isolated Areas:** Solo travelers should avoid venturing into isolated or unfamiliar areas, especially after dark. Stick to well-trafficked routes and places where other people are present. Ask locals or hotel staff for advice if you're unsure about a location.
- **Staying in Well-Lit Places:** Choosing well-lit streets and pathways when walking around urban areas at night. Avoid shortcuts through dark alleys or deserted parks, even if they seem to offer a quicker route.
- **Keeping Valuables Secure:** To reduce the risk of theft, use anti-theft bags or money belts that can be worn under your clothing. Keep your valuables, such as passports, cash, and electronics, secure and out of sight. Be mindful of your belongings when walking in crowded areas, as pick-pocketing can be a concern.

Using Public Transport Safely

Public transport is a convenient and affordable way to get around Thailand's cities, but it's important to stay alert and take precautions to ensure your safety while traveling alone.

Sitting Near the Driver:

- **On Buses or in Well-Lit Areas of Trains:** When using buses, try to sit near the driver or in areas with other passengers. On trains, choose carriages that are well-lit and occupied by other travelers. Avoid sitting in empty carriages or sections of the bus where you are isolated.

Avoiding Empty Carriages:

- **Traveling in Busier Sections:** If you find yourself in an empty train carriage, moving to a busier section is safer. Being surrounded by other passengers provides a level of safety and reduces the likelihood of unwanted attention.

Using Ride-Sharing Apps:

- **Booking Rides Through Reputable Apps Like Grab:** When taking taxis or ride-shares, use reputable apps like Grab, which offer the convenience of tracking your ride and ensuring that the driver has been vetted. You can avoid hailing taxis from the street, especially late at night. Always check that the license plate and driver's details match the information provided by the app before getting into the vehicle.

Safe Accommodation Practices

Choosing safe and secure accommodations is a crucial aspect of solo travel. Here's how to ensure that your stay is both comfortable and safe.

Choosing Reputable Hotels:

- **Reading Reviews and Checking Safety Features:** Before booking a hotel or hostel, read online reviews from other travelers, particularly those who have traveled solo. Look for accommodations with positive feedback regarding safety and security. Ensure the hotel has

CHAPTER 9: SAFETY TIPS FOR SOLO TRAVELERS

basic safety features such as secure door locks, 24-hour reception, and security cameras.

Securing the Room:

- **Using Door Locks and Safes for Valuables:** Once you've checked your room, ensure all door locks function correctly. If you're concerned about the room's security, use additional security measures like door wedges or portable locks. Store your valuables in the in-room safe or the hotel's secure deposit box if available.

Interacting with Staff:

- **Building Rapport and Seeking Their Advice:** Developing a good relationship with hotel staff can enhance safety. They can provide valuable local knowledge, such as avoiding areas and recommendations for safe dining and entertainment options. Don't hesitate to ask them for assistance or advice if you feel unsure about any aspect of your stay.

Safety Tips for Exploring Nightlife

Exploring the nightlife is a fun part of traveling, but taking extra precautions when you're on your own is important. Here are some tips to help you enjoy Thailand's vibrant nightlife while staying safe.

Staying in Groups:

- **Joining Other Travelers or Trusted Locals:** Whenever possible, go out with a group of fellow travelers or locals you trust. There is safety in numbers, and being part of a group can help deter unwanted attention. If you're going out alone, consider joining a group tour or organized event where you can meet others in a safe environment.

Watching Drinks:

- **Avoiding Leaving Drinks Unattended:** Always keep an eye on your drink and never leave it unattended. If you need to step away, take your drink with you or ask someone you trust to watch it. To avoid the risk of drink spiking, ordering drinks directly from the bar and watching them being prepared is also a good idea.

Knowing Emergency Contacts:

- **Local Emergency Numbers and Hotel Address:** Before heading out, make sure you know the local emergency numbers (in Thailand, it's 191 for general emergencies and 1155 for the tourist police) and the address of your accommodation. It's also helpful to carry a card with your hotel's name, address, and phone number in English and Thai if you need to show it to a taxi driver or ask for directions.

Solo travel in Thailand can be an incredibly fulfilling experience, offering the chance to explore new places, meet new people, and discover yourself along the way. By staying vigilant and following these safety tips, you can navigate urban areas, use public transport, choose safe accommodations, and confidently enjoy nightlife. Remember, the key to a successful solo trip is always to be aware of your surroundings, trust your instincts, and take proactive steps to protect yourself. With the right precautions, you can enjoy all Thailand offers while staying safe and secure on your solo adventure.

Avoiding Common Scams and Tourist Traps

Traveling in Thailand can be an enriching experience, but like many popular tourist destinations, scams and tourist traps are unfortunately common. As a solo traveler, staying vigilant and informed is important *to avoid falling victim to these schemes. In this section, we'll explore some of the most common scams targeting tourists, provide tips on recognizing and avoiding them, offer advice on handling scam situations, and highlight tourist traps to avoid during your travels.*

Identifying Common Scams Targeting Tourists

Scams targeting tourists are often designed to exploit unfamiliarity with local customs and prices. Being aware of these scams is the first step in avoiding them.

Tuk-tuk Scams:

- **Overcharging and Taking Longer Routes:** Tuk-tuks are a popular mode of transport in Thailand but are also a common vehicle for scams. Drivers may offer a very

low fare initially, only to take you on a longer route or to unwanted destinations like gem shops or tailors, where they receive commissions. Alternatively, they may overcharge you significantly once the ride is over.
- **How to avoid this:** You can agree on a fare before starting your journey, or better yet, use a metered taxi or a ride-sharing app like Grab to avoid haggling altogether.

Traditional Tuk-Tuk

Gem Scams:

- **Being Sold Fake or Overpriced Gems:** One of the most infamous scams in Thailand involves being persuaded

to buy gems at a "special price" that can supposedly be sold for a profit back home. The gems are either fake or grossly overpriced, and the profit promised is a lie.
- **How to Avoid:** Avoid purchasing gems or jewelry unless you're at a reputable dealer. Be wary of anyone offering deals that sound too good to be true, especially if they involve significant amounts of money.

Fake Tour Guides:

- **Unofficial Guides Charging High Fees:** Some individuals pose as tour guides and offer their services at popular tourist attractions. These unofficial guides often charge exorbitant fees for subpar services or may take you to places where they receive commissions.
- **How to avoid this:** You can always book tours through reputable agencies or your hotel. Please ensure your guide is officially licensed, usually indicated by a badge or identification card.

Sob Story Scams:

- **People Asking for Money with Fabricated Stories:** Another common scam involves people approaching you with a sad story, asking for money to help them get back home, pay for a sick relative's treatment, or other emotional appeals. These stories are often fabricated to elicit sympathy and money from unsuspecting tourists.
- **How to Avoid:** It's best to decline and walk away politely. If you genuinely want to help those in need, consider donating to a reputable charity instead.

Tips for Recognizing and Avoiding Scams

Arming yourself with the right strategies can help you recognize and avoid scams before they happen.

Trusting Instincts:

- **Walking Away If Something Feels Off:** If a situation doesn't feel right, trust your gut instinct and remove yourself from it. Scammers often rely on creating a sense of urgency or pressure, so take a step back and evaluate the situation calmly.

Researching Prices:

- **Knowing Average Costs for Services:** Before heading out, research the typical costs for common services like tuk-tuk rides, tours, and food. Having a general idea of what things should cost will help you recognize when someone is trying to overcharge you.

Using Official Services:

- **Booking Tours and Transport Through Reputable Companies:** Whenever possible, book tours, transportation, and other services through reputable companies or your hotel. This minimizes the risk of falling victim to scams and ensures you receive the service you're paying for.

CHAPTER 9: SAFETY TIPS FOR SOLO TRAVELERS

How to Handle Scam Situations

Despite your best efforts, you may still encounter a scam situation. Knowing how to handle it calmly and effectively is essential.

Staying Calm:

- **Not Escalating the Situation:** If you realize you're being scammed, the most important thing is to stay calm. Getting angry or confrontational can escalate the situation, potentially putting you in more danger. Instead, try to exit the situation as smoothly as possible.

Reporting Scams:

- **Informing Local Authorities and Tourist Police:** After the incident, report the scam to local authorities or the tourist police. In Thailand, the tourist police can be reached by dialing 1155. While they may not always be able to recover your money, reporting helps raise awareness and may prevent others from being scammed.

Seeking Help:

- **From Hotel Staff and Trusted Locals:** If you're unsure whether something is a scam, seek advice from hotel staff or trusted locals before making any decisions. They can often provide insights into local customs and help you avoid potential scams.

Common Tourist Traps to Avoid

Tourist traps are designed to exploit visitors by charging inflated prices or providing subpar experiences. Here are some to watch out for.

Overpriced Souvenir Shops:

- **Avoiding Shops Near Major Attractions:** Souvenir shops near popular tourist attractions charge significantly more than shops in less touristy areas. They may also sell lower-quality goods.
- **How to Avoid:** Shop at local markets or stores away from major attractions. Prices are generally more reasonable, and you're more likely to find authentic items.

Tourist Restaurants:

- **Opting for Local Eateries Instead:** Restaurants located in tourist hot spots often cater to foreign tastes and charge higher prices, sometimes for lower-quality food.
- **How to Avoid:** To enjoy authentic Thai cuisine at a fair price, seek out local eateries or street food stalls or ask locals for recommendations.

Pushy Vendors:

- **Politely Declining and Walking Away:** Vendors in tourist areas can be persistent, trying to sell you souvenirs, tours, or other items. While they may be aggressive, it's important to remain polite.

- **How to Avoid:** If you're not interested, a firm but polite "No, thank you" followed by walking away is usually enough to deter further pressure.

Fake Charity Solicitations:

- **Checking Credentials Before Donating:** Some scammers pose as charity workers, asking for donations to causes that don't exist. They may have fake IDs or documents to make their operation seem legitimate.
- **How to Avoid:** If you're approached by someone asking for donations, politely ask for more information and verify their credentials. If in doubt, decline and consider donating to well-known, reputable organizations instead.

While Thailand is a beautiful and welcoming country, it's essential to stay aware of the potential for scams and tourist traps. By educating yourself about common scams, learning how to recognize and avoid them, and knowing how to handle situations if they arise, you can protect yourself and ensure your trip is safe and enjoyable. Remember, a little caution goes a long way in helping you navigate your travels confidently and avoid any unpleasant surprises.

Health and Wellness Tips for Solo Travelers

Maintaining your health and well-being while traveling is crucial, especially when you're exploring a new country on your own. As a solo traveler, it's important to be proactive about your physical and mental health to ensure that your journey is enjoyable and free from unnecessary complications. In this section, we'll cover essential health and wellness tips, including staying hydrated and eating safely, managing travel-related stress and fatigue, the importance of comprehensive travel insurance, and accessing healthcare services in Thailand.

Staying Hydrated and Eating Safely

One of the simplest yet most important aspects of staying healthy while traveling is ensuring that you remain properly hydrated and eat safely. Here's how to do that effectively in Thailand:

Drinking Bottled Water:

- **Avoiding Tap Water:** In Thailand, it's generally unsafe to drink tap water, as it may contain bacteria and other contaminants that can lead to illness. To stay hydrated, always opt for bottled water, which is widely available and affordable. Make sure the seal on the bottle is intact before drinking. If you stay in one place for an extended period, consider purchasing a large water jug to reduce plastic waste.

Eating at Busy Stalls:

- **Ensuring Food Turnover:** Street food is a highlight of visiting Thailand, but to minimize the risk of foodborne illness, it's wise to eat at busy stalls with a high turnover of food. This usually indicates that the food is fresh and has not been sitting out for long. Additionally, observe the stall's hygiene practices, such as whether the vendor is wearing gloves or using clean utensils.

Avoiding Raw Foods:

- **Especially Seafood and Unpeeled Fruits:** While Thai cuisine includes many delicious raw dishes, it's safer to avoid raw foods, particularly seafood, when eating at street stalls or lesser-known eateries. Raw seafood can carry a higher risk of food poisoning, especially in hot climates. Similarly, avoid eating unpeeled fruits and vegetables, as they may have been washed in contaminated water. Instead, choose fruits that can be peeled, like bananas or oranges, or eat at establishments where you trust the food preparation process.

Managing Travel-Related Stress and Fatigue

Traveling, especially on your own, can be both exhilarating and exhausting. Managing stress and fatigue is key to maintaining your mental and physical well-being throughout your journey.

Planning Rest Days:

- **Incorporating Downtime into Itineraries:** Getting caught up in exploring new places is easy, but scheduling rest days into your itinerary is essential. Allow yourself time to relax, whether it's lounging by the beach, enjoying a leisurely meal, or simply catching up on sleep. These breaks will help prevent burnout and energize you for the rest of your trip.

Practicing Mindfulness:

- **Meditation and Yoga:** Incorporating mindfulness practices like meditation and yoga into your daily routine can significantly reduce travel-related stress. These activities help you stay grounded, improve mental clarity, and enhance your overall sense of well-being. Many hotels and resorts in Thailand offer yoga classes, or you can practice alone in a quiet space.

Staying Connected:

- **Regular Check-ins with Family and Friends:** Staying in touch with loved ones back home can provide emotional support and help alleviate feelings of loneliness or anxiety. Schedule regular check-ins with family or friends, whether it's through a quick phone call, a video chat, or sharing updates on social media. This connection can be a great source of comfort and security while traveling solo.

The Significance of Travel Insurance

Travel insurance is a non-negotiable aspect of any trip, especially for solo travelers. Comprehensive travel insurance provides peace of mind by covering unexpected events that could otherwise derail your journey.

Emergency Medical Coverage:

- **Hospitalization and Evacuation:** Ensure that your travel insurance covers emergency medical situations, including hospitalization, treatment, and, if necessary, medical evacuation to your home country. This is particularly important if you plan to engage in activities with a higher risk of injury, such as trekking or scuba diving.

Trip Interruption:

- **Cancellations and Delays:** Life is unpredictable, and travel plans can change unexpectedly due to illness, weather, or other unforeseen circumstances. A good travel insurance policy should cover trip interruptions, including cancellations and delays, ensuring you're reimbursed for non-refundable expenses.

Activity Coverage:

- **Adventure Sports and Excursions:** If you plan to participate in adventure sports or other high-risk activities, ensure your insurance policy also covers them. Many standard policies exclude coverage for activities like diving, rock climbing, or zip-lining, so checking and possibly purchasing additional coverage is essential.

Accessing Healthcare Services in Thailand

While Thailand has a robust healthcare system, accessing medical care can still be daunting, especially if you're in a rural area or facing a language barrier. Here's how to navigate healthcare services as a solo traveler:

Finding Hospitals and Clinics:

- **Major Cities vs. Rural Areas:** In major cities like Bangkok, Chiang Mai, and Phuket, you'll find many hospitals and clinics, including international-standard facilities with English-speaking staff. However, in rural areas, healthcare options may be more limited, and language barriers can be more pronounced. Researching the nearest medical facilities to your destination is a good idea before you travel.

Carrying a First Aid Kit:

- **Basic Supplies and Medications:** A well-stocked first aid kit is a must for any solo traveler. Include basic supplies like bandages, antiseptic wipes, pain relievers, and prescription medications. It's also wise to carry medications for common travel ailments like diarrhea, motion sickness, and allergies.

Overcoming Language Barriers:

- **Using Translation Apps and Seeking English-Speaking Doctors:** Language barriers can be challenging when seeking medical care in Thailand. Use translation apps like Google Translate to communicate your symptoms and needs to overcome these. Also, in larger hospitals, please ask for an English-speaking doctor to ensure you receive accurate and appropriate care.

Staying healthy and well is fundamental to maximizing your solo travel experience in Thailand. By staying hydrated, eating safely, managing stress, ensuring comprehensive travel insurance, and knowing how to access healthcare, you can protect yourself from many common travel-related issues. Prioritizing your health and well-being helps you enjoy your journey to the fullest and ensures that you return home with nothing but positive memories of your adventure.

CHAPTER 10: OUTDOOR ADVENTURES

Thailand is a paradise for outdoor enthusiasts, offering diverse adventures that allow you to connect with nature in its most pristine form. From dense jungles teeming with wildlife to breathtaking mountain landscapes, the country's natural beauty is best experienced through jungle trekking and wildlife safaris. This chapter will guide you through the thrills of exploring Thailand's wilderness, highlighting popular trekking routes and wildlife safari destinations and providing essential tips for safe and responsible travel.

Jungle Trekking and Wildlife Safaris

Jungle trekking in Thailand offers an unparalleled opportunity to experience the country's rich biodiversity and stunning landscapes. Whether navigating the dense forests of the north, exploring the tropical rainforests of the south, or walking historical trails in central Thailand, each region provides unique trekking experiences.

CHAPTER 10: OUTDOOR ADVENTURES

Northern Thailand:

- **Dense Forests and Hill Tribe Villages:** The mountainous regions of Northern Thailand are home to some of the country's most iconic trekking routes. Trekking here often involves visiting remote hill tribe villages, where you can learn about the traditional ways of life of the Karen, Hmong, Lahu, and other ethnic groups. The cool climate and lush landscapes make this region a favorite among trekkers.

Southern Thailand:

- **Tropical Rainforests and National Parks:** Southern Thailand's treks are characterized by lush, tropical rainforests and stunning national parks. These treks often lead you through ancient forests, past towering limestone cliffs, and to hidden waterfalls. This region's diversity of flora and fauna is remarkable, offering a true jungle adventure.

Central Thailand:

- **Diverse Flora and Fauna, Historical Trails:** Central Thailand offers a mix of dense jungles and historical trails that often trace the routes of ancient civilizations. This region is ideal for those looking to combine natural beauty with cultural exploration, as many trails pass through historic sites and along rivers that have played significant roles in Thailand's history.

Seasonal Considerations:

- **Best Times to Trek and Weather Impacts:** The best time to go jungle trekking in Thailand is during the cool season (November to February), when temperatures are more moderate, and the risk of heavy rains is lower. The hot season (March to May) can be challenging due to high temperatures, while the rainy season (June to October) can make trails slippery and more difficult to navigate, but it also brings lush green landscapes and fuller waterfalls.

Popular Trekking Routes and Destinations

Thailand's trekking routes offer something for every level of adventurer, from multi-day treks in the north to day hikes in lush national parks.

Chiang Mai to Mae Hong Son:

- **Multi-Day Treks and Hill Tribe Visits:** This popular trekking route takes you through the mountainous regions of Northern Thailand, offering the opportunity to visit hill tribe villages and experience the local culture. The trek usually lasts several days, with overnight stays in village homestays. Along the way, you'll trek through dense forests, cross rivers, and climb to mountain viewpoints with breathtaking vistas.

CHAPTER 10: OUTDOOR ADVENTURES

Khao Sok National Park:

- **Dense Rainforest and Ancient Trees:** Located in southern Thailand, Khao Sok National Park is one of the country's most beautiful natural reserves. The park is home to some of the oldest rainforests in the world, with towering trees, limestone cliffs, and abundant wildlife. Treks in Khao Sok can range from easy day hikes to more challenging multi-day adventures, often including boat trips on the park's stunning Cheow Lan Lake.

Khao Sok National Park

Umphang Wildlife Sanctuary:

- **Thi Lo Su Waterfall and Remote Trails:** Umphang, located near the Myanmar border, is one of Thailand's most remote trekking destinations. The sanctuary is famous for Thi Lo Su Waterfall, Thailand's largest and most spectacular waterfall. Treks in Umphang are typically more challenging, involving several days of hiking through dense jungle and crossing rivers, but the remote beauty of the area makes it well worth the effort.

Wildlife Safaris and What to Expect

Thailand's national parks offer exciting safari opportunities for those who prefer to observe wildlife in its natural habitat. These safaris provide a chance to see some of the country's most iconic wildlife, including elephants, gibbons, and various bird species.

Khao Yai National Park:

- **Elephants, Gibbons, and Bird Watching:** Khao Yai, Thailand's oldest national park, is a UNESCO World Heritage site and one of the best places in the country for wildlife spotting. The park is home to wild elephants, gibbons, deer, and numerous bird species. Guided safaris offer the chance to see these animals in their natural environment, with early morning and late afternoon being the best times for wildlife viewing.

CHAPTER 10: OUTDOOR ADVENTURES

Kui Buri National Park:

- **Wild Elephants and Gaurs:** Kui Buri, located in the Prachuap Khiri Khan Province, is renowned for its wild elephant population. It's one of the few places in Thailand where you can almost guarantee to see these majestic creatures. The park also hosts other wildlife, such as gaurs (a type of wild cattle) and various bird species. Safaris in Kui Buri are typically conducted in open-top vehicles, providing an immersive experience.

Kui Buri National Park

Kaeng Krachan National Park:

- **Diverse Wildlife and Bird Species:** Kaeng Krachan, Thailand's largest national park, is a haven for wildlife enthusiasts. The park's diverse ecosystems range from lowland rainforests to mountainous terrain, supporting various species. Visitors can spot elephants, leopards, gibbons, and an impressive array of birds. The park's remote location means it's less crowded, offering a more serene and undisturbed wildlife experience.

Tips for Safe and Responsible Trekking and Safaris

Whether you're trekking through the jungle or embarking on a wildlife safari, preparation and respect for the environment are key to a safe and enjoyable experience.

Hiring Local Guides:

- **Expertise and Safety:** Hiring a local guide is essential for navigating Thailand's jungles and understanding its wildlife. Local guides have extensive knowledge of the terrain, flora, and fauna and can enhance your experience by providing insights you might miss. They also ensure your safety, particularly on challenging trails or during encounters with wildlife.

CHAPTER 10: OUTDOOR ADVENTURES

Packing Essentials:

- **Proper Footwear, Insect Repellent, and First Aid Kit:** When trekking, it's important to wear sturdy, comfortable footwear that can handle rough terrain. Insect repellent is a must, as mosquitoes and other insects are common in Thailand's jungles. Carry a basic first aid kit with essentials like bandages, antiseptic wipes, and any personal medications you may need. Don't forget a hat, sunscreen, and plenty of water to stay hydrated.

Environmental Respect:

- **Leave No Trace and Wildlife Protection:** Always practice Leave No Trace principles while trekking or on safari. This means taking all your trash with you, staying on designated trails, and avoiding disturbing wildlife. Respect the animals by keeping a safe distance and not feeding them, as this can disrupt their natural behaviors and make them reliant on human food.

Physical Preparation:

- **Fitness Levels and Acclimatization:** Some treks in Thailand can be physically demanding, so it's important to assess your fitness level before embarking on a journey. If you're planning a challenging trek, spend some time acclimatizing to the local climate and altitude, especially in mountainous regions. Regular exercise and a few practice hikes before your trip can also help you prepare.

Outdoor adventures in Thailand offer an unforgettable way to experience the country's natural beauty and rich biodiversity. Whether you're trekking through remote jungles, visiting hill tribe villages, or spotting wildlife in national parks, these activities provide a deeper connection to the land and its inhabitants. Following the tips in this chapter, you can enjoy these adventures safely and responsibly, ensuring that you leave with incredible memories and a greater appreciation for Thailand's wild places.

Diving and Snorkeling Hot-spots

Thailand is a paradise above ground, offering an underwater world teeming with vibrant marine life, crystal-clear waters, and some of the world's best diving and snorkeling spots. Whether you're a seasoned diver or a first-time snorkeler, the waters surrounding Thailand's islands and coastal regions provide a rich and diverse experience that will leave a lasting impression. This section will explore Thailand's top diving and snorkeling hot spots, describe what you can expect to see, and provide tips for safe and responsible underwater exploration.

The Underwater World of Thailand

Thailand's underwater ecosystems are renowned for their stunning biodiversity and colorful coral reefs. The warm waters of the Andaman Sea and the Gulf of Thailand create ideal conditions for diving and snorkeling, attracting marine enthusiasts from all over the globe.

CHAPTER 10: OUTDOOR ADVENTURES

Coral Reefs:

- **Vibrant Marine Life and Coral Conservation:** Thailand's coral reefs are some of the most diverse in the world, home to many marine species, including fish, crustaceans, and mollusks. These reefs are crucial to the health of marine ecosystems, and there are ongoing conservation efforts to protect and restore them. While diving or snorkeling, you'll witness the vibrant life these reefs support, from schools of colorful fish to the intricate beauty of the corals themselves.

Clear Waters:

- **Visibility and Ideal Conditions:** Thailand's waters are known for their excellent visibility, often exceeding 30 meters in some areas, making it easier to explore the underwater world. The calm seas, especially during the dry season (November to April), create perfect conditions for both diving and snorkeling, ensuring a safe and enjoyable experience.

Marine Species:

- **Turtles, Sharks, and Colorful Fish:** The waters around Thailand are home to a rich array of marine species. You might encounter gentle sea turtles gliding through the water, graceful reef sharks patrolling the coral gardens, and countless species of vibrant, colorful fish darting among the coral. The biodiversity here is astonishing, offering endless opportunities for underwater exploration.

Popular Diving Destinations

Thailand is famous for its world-class diving sites, each offering unique experiences for divers of all levels. Here are some of the top diving destinations you shouldn't miss.

Similan Islands:

- **World-Renowned Dive Sites and Live-aboard Trips:** The Similan Islands, located off the west coast of Thailand in the Andaman Sea, are consistently ranked among the top dive sites in the world. The islands are known for their stunning underwater rock formations, vibrant coral reefs, and diverse marine life. Diving here often involves live-aboard trips, where you can spend several days exploring the various dive sites, such as Elephant Head Rock, Richelieu Rock, and Christmas Point. Expect to see everything from manta rays and whale sharks to macro life like nudibranchs and sea horses.

Koh Tao:

- **Diving Schools and Beginner-Friendly Sites:** Koh Tao, located in the Gulf of Thailand, is the country's most popular destination for learning to dive. The island is home to numerous diving schools that offer PADI certification courses, making it an ideal spot for beginners. The dive sites around Koh Tao are relatively shallow and easy to navigate, with highlights including Chumphon Pinnacle, Shark Island, and the Japanese Gardens. The island's calm waters and excellent visibility make it perfect for novice divers seeking experience.

Koh Tao Sunset

Richelieu Rock:

- **Whale Sharks and Diverse Marine Life:** Richelieu Rock, part of the Surin Islands, is one of Thailand's most famous dive sites, particularly known for its whale shark sightings. The site is a submerged pinnacle located in the Andaman Sea, offering a dramatic underwater landscape teeming with life. In addition to whale sharks, divers can expect to see large schools of pelagic fish, barracudas, jacks, and various species of rays. The diversity of marine life here makes it a must-visit for experienced divers.

Snorkeling Spots and What to Expect

For those who prefer to stay closer to the surface, Thailand's snorkeling spots offer incredible opportunities to explore the country's marine life without deep diving.

Phi Phi Islands:

- **Shallow Reefs and Colorful Fish:** The Phi Phi Islands in the Andaman Sea are famous for their crystal-clear waters and stunning limestone cliffs. The shallow reefs around the islands are ideal for snorkeling, with vibrant coral gardens and many colorful fish beneath the surface. Popular snorkeling spots include Bamboo Island, Monkey Beach, and Maya Bay (when open). The calm waters and abundant marine life make the Phi Phi Islands a top snorkeler choice.

Phi-Phi Islands

Koh Lanta:

- **Coral Gardens and Snorkeling Tours:** Koh Lanta, also located in the Andaman Sea, offers some of the best snorkeling in Thailand. The island is surrounded by beautiful coral gardens, particularly around the smaller islands of Koh Rok and Koh Haa. Snorkeling tours often include visits to these sites, where you can swim among pristine corals and observe a diverse range of marine species, from parrot and clown fish to sea turtles and rays.

Ao Nang:

- **Accessible Sites and Diverse Ecosystems:** Ao Nang, located on the mainland near Krabi, is a gateway to numerous excellent snorkeling spots. The nearby islands of Poda, Chicken, and Tub offer easy access to vibrant coral reefs and clear waters. Ao Nang is particularly well-suited for travelers who want to combine beach time with snorkeling, as many of the best sites are just a short boat ride away. The area's diverse marine ecosystems provide plenty to explore, from shallow reefs to deeper waters.

Tips for Safe and Enjoyable Diving and Snorkeling

It's essential to be well-prepared and follow best practices to ensure a safe and enjoyable experience while exploring Thailand's underwater world.

Certification:

- **PADI Courses and Diving Schools:** If you plan to dive, ensure you're properly certified. Thailand is home to numerous PADI-certified diving schools that offer courses for all levels, from beginner to advanced. Completing a course ensures that you have the necessary skills and knowledge to dive safely.

CHAPTER 10: OUTDOOR ADVENTURES

Gear Essentials:

- **Masks, Fins, Snorkels, and Wet Suits:** Whether you're diving or snorkeling, having the right gear is essential. Ensure that your mask fits well, provides a clear view, and that your fins are comfortable and appropriately sized. A dry snorkel is a good investment if you're snorkeling, as it prevents water from entering the tube. A wet suit is recommended for diving, particularly if you're diving in cooler waters or spending extended time underwater.

Marine Conservation:

- **Avoiding Coral Damage and Respecting Marine Life:** Practicing responsible marine conservation is crucial when diving or snorkeling. Avoid touching or stepping on corals, as they are fragile and can be easily damaged. Never feed or chase marine animals; keep a safe distance to avoid disturbing their natural behaviors. Participating in Eco-friendly diving or snorkeling tours that prioritize conservation is a great way to enjoy the underwater world while helping to protect it.

Safety Practices:

- **Buddy System and Checking Weather Conditions:** Always dive or snorkel with a buddy for added safety. Before heading out, check the weather conditions and tide schedules to ensure a safe experience. If you're new to diving or snorkeling, consider joining a guided tour where an experienced guide can assist and provide additional safety measures.

Thailand's underwater landscapes are as captivating as its terrestrial ones, offering unforgettable diving and snorkeling experiences catering to all expertise levels. Whether you're swimming with whale sharks at Richelieu Rock, exploring the coral gardens of Koh Lanta, or learning to dive on Koh Tao, the country's rich marine biodiversity promises a unique adventure. By following the tips in this chapter, you can enjoy these activities safely and responsibly, ensuring that you and the delicate marine ecosystems remain protected. Dive in and explore the wonders that lie beneath the surface of Thailand's stunning waters!

Rock Climbing and Waterfall Exploration

Thailand's natural beauty isn't just confined to its beaches and jungles; the country is also a paradise for outdoor adventurers who seek the thrill of rock climbing and the serene beauty of waterfalls. With its towering limestone cliffs and majestic waterfalls, Thailand offers unique experiences that attract climbers and nature lovers worldwide. In this section, we'll delve into the appeal of rock climbing in Thailand, highlight top climbing destinations, explore some of the country's most breathtaking waterfalls, and provide essential tips for safe and enjoyable outdoor adventures.

CHAPTER 10: OUTDOOR ADVENTURES

Rock Climbing in Thailand

Thailand has become a world-renowned destination for rock climbing, thanks to its dramatic limestone cliffs, varied climbing routes, and vibrant climbing culture. Whether you're an experienced climber or a beginner looking to try something new, Thailand offers something for everyone.

Limestone Cliffs:

- **Unique Formations and Challenging Routes:** The limestone cliffs that line Thailand's coast and inland areas are visually stunning and provide an array of climbing challenges. These cliffs, with their unique formations of stalactites, overhangs, and caves, offer routes that cater to all skill levels—from easy climbs for beginners to advanced routes that test even the most seasoned climbers.

Popular Climbing Spots:

- **Coastal Cliffs and Inland Crags:** Thailand's rock climbing scene is diverse, with popular spots scattered across both coastal and inland regions. Coastal cliffs like those at Railay and Tonsai beaches in Krabi are famous for their beauty and accessibility, while inland crags around Chiang Mai offer a different climbing experience amid lush forests and mountainous terrain.

Climbing Culture:

- **International Community and Climbing Schools:** Thailand's rock climbing spots are hubs for an international climbing community. Here, you'll find climbing schools and experienced instructors who offer courses and guided climbs for all levels. This welcoming environment makes it easy for newcomers to get started and for seasoned climbers to find partners and new challenges.

Popular Rock Climbing Destinations

Thailand is home to some of the world's most iconic climbing destinations, each offering unique routes and stunning natural backdrops.

Railay Beach (Krabi):

- **Famous Climbing Mecca and Diverse Routes:** Railay Beach, located in Krabi Province, is perhaps Thailand's most famous rock climbing destination. The area is known for its sheer limestone cliffs that rise dramatically from the sea, offering over 700 routes that range from beginner-friendly to extremely challenging. The picturesque setting, with turquoise waters and white sandy beaches, makes climbing at Railay an unforgettable experience. Popular spots include Phra Nang Cave Beach and Tonsai Tower, both of which offer breathtaking views and a variety of climbing challenges.

Railay Beach

Chiang Mai:

- **Doi Chiang Dao and Crazy Horse Buttress:** Chiang Mai, located in Northern Thailand, is another top climbing destination. Doi Chiang Dao, Thailand's third-highest peak, offers adventurous multi-pitch climbs with stunning panoramic views. Meanwhile, Crazy Horse Buttress, just outside Chiang Mai city, is a well-developed climbing area with routes for all skill levels. This area is known for its excellent limestone walls, caves, and the solid local climbing community that maintains the crags and supports new climbers.

Tonsai Beach:

- **Advanced Routes and Climbing Community:** Adjacent to Railay Beach, Tonsai Beach is a haven for more experienced climbers seeking challenging routes. The area is known for its steep, overhanging climbs and deep water soloing opportunities. Tonsai has a laid-back, bohemian vibe, attracting climbers worldwide who come for the tough routes and stay for the community. Routes like Cobra Wall and Cat Wall offer some of the most challenging climbs in the region, set against a backdrop of stunning coastal scenery.

Waterfall Exploration in Thailand

Beyond its beaches and cliffs, Thailand is also home to some of the most beautiful waterfalls in Southeast Asia. Exploring these waterfalls offers a chance to cool off in natural pools, hike through lush jungles, and experience the serene beauty of Thailand's natural landscapes.

Erawan Waterfall (Kanchanaburi):

- **Multi-Tiered Falls and Swimming Spots:** Located in Erawan National Park, Erawan Waterfall is one of Thailand's most famous waterfalls. The waterfall has seven tiers, each with its own unique pools and cascades. Visitors can hike up to the higher tiers, enjoying the increasingly beautiful views and tranquil swimming spots along the way. The clear, emerald-green pools at the base of each tier are perfect for a refreshing dip, making

Erawan a popular day trip from Bangkok.

Erawan Waterfall

Thi Lo Su Waterfall (Tak):

- **Largest Waterfall in Thailand and Remote Access:** Thi Lo Su, located in Umphang Wildlife Sanctuary in Tak Province, is the largest waterfall in Thailand and one of the most spectacular. The waterfall is 300 meters high and nearly 500 meters wide, cascading over multiple tiers. Its remote location adds to its allure, as getting there requires a combination of driving, trekking, and rafting. The effort is well worth it, as Thi Lo Su offers an awe-inspiring experience of nature's power and beauty.

Haew Suwat Waterfall (Khao Yai):

- **Famous Filming Location and Scenic Views:** Haew Suwat Waterfall, located in Khao Yai National Park, gained fame as a filming location for the movie "The Beach." This picturesque waterfall drops about 20 meters into a large pool below, surrounded by lush greenery. It's easily accessible from the park's main roads, making it a popular spot for visitors to Khao Yai. The area around the waterfall offers scenic viewpoints and short hikes, making it a perfect stop for nature lovers.

Tips for Safe and Enjoyable Rock Climbing and Waterfall Exploration

Whether you're scaling cliffs or exploring waterfalls, safety should always be a top priority. Here are some essential tips to ensure a safe and enjoyable adventure.

Climbing Safety:

- **Harnesses, Ropes, and Belaying Techniques:** Always use proper climbing gear, including harnesses, ropes, and helmets. If you're new to climbing or attempting a difficult route, consider hiring a certified guide to ensure that you're using the correct belaying techniques and that your gear is properly set up. Safety checks should be routine before every climb, and communication with your climbing partner is key to avoiding accidents.

CHAPTER 10: OUTDOOR ADVENTURES

Hiring Guides:

- **Local Expertise and Safety Assurance:** Hiring a local guide can greatly enhance your climbing or waterfall exploration experience. Guides ensure your safety and provide valuable knowledge about the best routes, local conditions, and the natural environment. In remote or challenging areas, a guide's expertise can be crucial.

Waterfall Safety:

- **Slippery Rocks and Swimming Precautions:** Waterfalls can be dangerous if proper precautions aren't taken. Rocks around waterfalls are often slippery, so wear shoes with good grip and watch your step. Be aware of the water's depth and current when swimming, and avoid diving into unknown areas. Always respect warning signs and avoid swimming during heavy rains or solid currents.

Environmental Respect:

- **No Littering and Preserving Natural Beauty:** As with any outdoor activity, leaving no trace is essential. Pack out all trash, avoid disturbing wildlife, and stick to established paths to prevent erosion and protect the natural environment. When climbing, avoid damaging the rock face or surrounding vegetation. Your respect for the environment helps ensure that these natural wonders remain pristine for future visitors.

Thailand's rock climbing and waterfall exploration opportunities offer thrilling and beautiful ways to connect with nature. Whether climbing the iconic Railay Beach cliffs, hiking to the majestic Thi Lo Su Waterfall, or simply enjoying the serenity of a lesser-known crag or cascade, these outdoor adventures provide unforgettable experiences. By following the tips in this chapter, you can ensure that your exploration of Thailand's natural wonders is safe and responsible, leaving you with memories that will last a lifetime.

CHAPTER 11: ROMANTIC GETAWAYS

Romantic Getaways

With its stunning landscapes, tranquil beaches, and luxurious resorts, Thailand is the perfect destination for a romantic getaway. Whether you're seeking the serenity of a secluded beach or the indulgence of a luxury resort, Thailand offers countless opportunities for couples to create unforgettable memories together. In this chapter, we'll explore some of the most romantic destinations in Thailand, highlighting secluded beaches, luxurious resorts, and special activities designed to enhance your romantic escape.

Secluded Beaches for Couples

For couples seeking privacy and a tranquil atmosphere, Thailand's lesser-known beaches offer the perfect setting for intimate moments. Far from the crowded tourist spots, these hidden gems provide the ideal backdrop for romance.

Ao Leuk Bay (Koh Tao):

- **Crystal-Clear Waters and Quiet Shores:** Ao Leuk Bay, located on the eastern side of Koh Tao, is a serene and less crowded beach, perfect for couples looking for a peaceful retreat. The bay is known for its crystal-clear waters and vibrant coral reefs, making it an ideal spot for snorkeling and swimming. The soft, white sand and calm atmosphere create the perfect setting for a romantic beach day.

Haad Yuan (Koh Phangan):

- **Remote Location and Peaceful Atmosphere:** Haad Yuan is a remote beach on Koh Phangan, accessible only by boat or a challenging hike through the jungle. Its secluded location ensures it remains peaceful and quiet, even during the peak tourist season. The beach's natural beauty, with its lush green backdrop and turquoise waters, makes it an ideal spot for couples to relax and enjoy each other's company.

CHAPTER 11: ROMANTIC GETAWAYS

Koh-Phangan

Sunset Beach (Koh Lipe):

- **Breathtaking Sunsets and Tranquil Setting:** As the name suggests, Sunset Beach on Koh Lipe offers some of Thailand's most stunning sunset views. This small, quiet beach on the island's western side is perfect for couples looking to unwind and watch the sun dip below the horizon. The tranquil setting, combined with the beautiful colors of the sunset, creates a magical atmosphere for romance.

173

Romantic Activities for Couples at Secluded Beaches

Once you've found your perfect beach escape, plenty of romantic activities can be enjoyed together.

Beach Picnics:

- **Secluded Spots and Local Delicacies:** Pack a picnic with local Thai delicacies and find a quiet spot on the beach to enjoy a meal together. Many local markets offer fresh fruits, snacks, and drinks that you can take with you. Some resorts also offer picnic services, where they prepare everything for you, allowing you to focus on the moment.

Sunset Watching:

- **Ideal Viewpoints and Best Times:** Find the perfect spot to watch the sunset, whether it's from a rocky outcrop, a beachside hammock, or directly on the sand. The best time to catch the sunset is usually around 6 PM, but it's worth arriving early to find your spot and enjoy the changing colors of the sky as the sun sets.

Snorkeling:

- **Coral Reefs and Marine Life:** Take advantage of the clear waters and vibrant coral reefs at these secluded beaches by going snorkeling. Share the experience of discovering colorful fish, sea turtles, and other marine life as you explore the underwater world together.

CHAPTER 11: ROMANTIC GETAWAYS

Beach Walks:

- **Scenic Routes and Photo Opportunities:** A stroll along the beach at sunrise or sunset can be incredibly romantic. Walk hand in hand along the shore, take in the scenic views, and capture the moment with some photos to remember your special time together.

Tips for Accessing These Hidden Gems

Reaching these secluded beaches may require a bit more effort, but the reward is well worth it. Here's how to get there:

Boat Transfers:

- **Private Charters and Scheduled Ferries:** Many secluded beaches are accessible only by boat. You can either book a private charter for a more exclusive experience or take a scheduled ferry that connects the main island to these hidden gems. Private charters offer flexibility in timing and routes, while ferries are a more budget-friendly option.

Local Transportation:

- **Renting Scooters and Tuk-Tuks:** If your secluded beach is accessible by road, consider renting a scooter or taking a tuk-tuk to get there. Renting a scooter allows you to explore the island at your own pace, while a tuk-tuk ride offers a fun and authentic way to travel.

Tuk-Tuk

Walking Trails:

- **Pathways and Difficulty Levels:** Some beaches, like Haad Yuan, are reachable by hiking trails. These trails can vary in difficulty, so it's important to wear appropriate footwear and be prepared for a bit of a trek. The journey through the jungle or along coastal paths adds to the adventure and makes the destination even more rewarding.

CHAPTER 11: ROMANTIC GETAWAYS

Nearby Accommodations

To complete your romantic getaway, staying at a nearby romantic and comfortable accommodation is essential. Here are some top choices:

Boutique Hotels:

- **Personalized Service and Unique Decor:** Boutique hotels near these secluded beaches offer personalized service and charming decor, often reflecting the local culture and natural surroundings. These smaller establishments provide a more intimate and cozy experience for couples.

Beachfront Bungalows:

- **Direct Beach Access and Private Balconies:** For a truly immersive experience, consider staying in a beachfront bungalow. These accommodations often offer direct access to the beach and private balconies to enjoy the ocean views in complete privacy. Many bungalows are designed to blend in with the natural environment, enhancing the feeling of being in a romantic hideaway.

Eco-Resorts:

- **Sustainable Practices and Natural Settings:** Eco-resorts near these beaches are a great option for couples who want to enjoy luxury while minimizing their environmental impact. These resorts typically use sustainable practices, such as solar energy and locally sourced materials, and are often set in beautiful, natural surroundings that emphasize the connection with nature.

Luxurious Resorts and Spas

For those seeking the ultimate luxury and romance, Thailand's top resorts offer unparalleled experiences that cater to couples.

The Sarojin (Khao Lak):

- **Private Pool Villas and Beachfront Dining:** The Sarojin is a luxury boutique resort in Khao Lak, renowned for its romantic ambiance and exceptional service. Couples can stay in private pool villas, dine on the beach under the stars, and enjoy personalized excursions designed for two. The resort's lush gardens and secluded setting create an intimate atmosphere perfect for honeymooners and couples celebrating special occasions.

CHAPTER 11: ROMANTIC GETAWAYS

Khao-Lak

Six Senses Yao Noi (Koh Yao Noi):

- **Stunning Views and Eco-Luxury:** Six Senses Yao Noi, located on the tranquil island of Koh Yao Noi, offers breathtaking views of Phang Nga Bay and an Eco-friendly approach to luxury. The resort features spacious villas with private pools, open-air bathrooms, and panoramic views. Couples can indulge in private dining experiences, sunset cruises, and wellness treatments in the resort's serene surroundings.

Rayavadee (Krabi):

- **Unique Location and Luxury Amenities:** Nestled in a stunning location between Railay Beach and Phra Nang Cave Beach, Rayavadee offers a unique blend of luxury and natural beauty. Lush tropical gardens and limestone cliffs surround the resort's pavilions and villas. Guests can enjoy private dinners on the beach, relax in the luxurious spa, and explore the nearby islands on a private boat tour.

Krabi-Railay Beach

Luxurious Amenities and Services

These luxury resorts offer a range of high-end amenities and services designed to enhance the romantic experience.

Private Plunge Pools:

- **Secluded Swimming and Ocean Views:** Many luxury resorts offer private plunge pools with stunning ocean views, providing a secluded space where couples can relax and enjoy each other's company. These pools are often surrounded by lush vegetation, ensuring complete privacy.

Couple's Massages:

- **In-Room or Spa, Professional Therapists:** Indulge in a couple's massage, either in the privacy of your villa or at the resort's spa. Professional therapists use traditional Thai techniques and aromatic oils to provide a deeply relaxing experience that you can share with your partner.

Candlelit Dinners:

- Beachside, Customized Menus: A romantic candlelit dinner on the beach is a must-do for couples staying at a luxury resort. Many resorts offer customized menus featuring local and international cuisine paired with fine wines and served under the stars. Whether it's a special occasion or a spontaneous romantic gesture, this experience will indeed create lasting memories.

Private Excursions:

- **Sunset Cruises and Island Hopping:** Luxury resorts often offer private excursions, such as sunset cruises or island-hopping tours. These excursions are designed to be intimate and personalized, allowing couples to explore Thailand's beautiful islands and waters in complete privacy.

Spa Treatments and Wellness Experiences

A romantic getaway wouldn't be complete without indulging in some rejuvenating spa treatments and wellness experiences.

Traditional Thai Massages:

- **Relaxation Techniques and Skilled Practitioners:** A traditional Thai massage is a deeply relaxing experience that combines acupressure, stretching, and rhythmic movements. Many luxury resorts offer this treatment as part of their wellness programs, allowing couples to unwind and relax together.

Aromatherapy Sessions:

- **Essential Oils and Calming Environment:** Aromatherapy sessions use essential oils to promote relaxation and well-being. Couples can enjoy these sessions in a tranquil setting, often accompanied by soothing music and a calming atmosphere.

Herbal Steam Baths:

- **Detoxifying and Rejuvenating:** Herbal steam baths are a traditional Thai wellness practice that detoxifies the body and rejuvenates the skin. Many luxury resorts offer this treatment in their spa facilities, providing couples with a unique and refreshing experience.

Yoga and Meditation Classes:

- **Beachfront Settings and Private Sessions:** Yoga and meditation are perfect activities for couples looking to connect on a deeper level. Many resorts offer private classes in beachfront settings, allowing couples to practice together while enjoying Thailand's natural beauty.

Tips for Booking and Making the Most of Luxury Stays

To ensure that your romantic getaway is as perfect as possible, here are some tips for booking and maximizing your luxury experience.

Special Packages:

- **Honeymoon Deals and All-Inclusive Offers:** Many luxury resorts offer special packages designed for couples, such as honeymoon deals or all-inclusive offers that include meals, spa treatments, and excursions. These packages often provide added value and make planning your getaway easier.

Early Booking:

- **Securing the Best Rooms and Discounts:** To get the best rates and ensure availability, it's recommended that you book your stay well in advance. Early booking often offers discounts and lets you choose the best rooms or villas.

Personal Requests:

- **Customizing Stays and Special Arrangements:** Don't hesitate to communicate any special requests or preferences when booking your stay. Whether it's arranging a surprise for your partner, setting up a private dinner, or customizing your room's amenities, the resort staff will usually go out of their way to accommodate your needs.

Resort Activities:

- **Scheduling and Participation:** Take advantage of the resort's activities, such as cooking classes, guided tours, or wellness workshops. These activities are often designed to enhance your stay and provide unique experiences that you can enjoy together as a couple.

Thailand is a dream destination for couples seeking romance, whether you're drawn to the serene beauty of secluded beaches or the indulgent luxury of world-class resorts. Following this chapter's suggestions, you can create a romantic getaway tailored to your desires, filled with unforgettable moments and cherished memories. Whether celebrating a honeymoon, an anniversary, or simply spending quality time together, Thailand's romantic offerings will surely provide the perfect backdrop for your love story.

Unique Romantic Activities

Thailand's diverse landscapes, rich culture, and warm hospitality provide the perfect backdrop for romantic experiences that go beyond the ordinary. Whether you're celebrating a special occasion or simply looking to create unforgettable memories with your partner, the country offers many unique activities that foster deep connections and lasting impressions. In this section, we'll explore some of Thailand's most memorable romantic activities, *from breathtaking hot air balloon rides to intimate dining experiences, and provide tips on personalizing these moments to make them even more special.*

Unique and Memorable Activities for Couples

Thailand is brimming with activities that allow couples to share new experiences and deepen their connection in extraordinary settings.

Hot Air Balloon Rides (Chiang Mai):

- **Scenic Flights and Sunrise Views:** For a truly unforgettable experience, consider taking a hot air balloon ride over the lush landscapes of Chiang Mai. Floating gently above the countryside at sunrise, you'll be treated to panoramic views of mist-covered mountains, rice paddies, and ancient temples. The serene silence of the early morning, coupled with the breathtaking scenery, creates a magical atmosphere that's perfect for romance. Many balloon companies offer packages that include a post-flight champagne breakfast, adding an extra touch of luxury to the experience.

Hot Air Balloon Ride

Private Cooking Classes:

- **Learning Thai Cuisine in an Intimate Setting:** Sharing a private cooking class is a wonderful way for couples to bond while learning something new. In the comfort of a traditional Thai kitchen or even in your resort's outdoor pavilion, you'll be guided by a professional chef through the process of creating classic Thai dishes. From selecting fresh ingredients at a local market to mastering the art of Thai curry, this hands-on experience allows you to work together and enjoy the fruits of your labor in a romantic meal you've prepared yourselves.

Long-Tail Boat Tours:

- **Exploring Hidden Caves and Private Beaches:** Discover Thailand's hidden gems with a private long-tail boat tour. These traditional wooden boats can take you to secluded beaches, hidden caves, and pristine islands that are often inaccessible by larger vessels. You can customize your itinerary to include stops at private beaches where you can enjoy a picnic, snorkel in crystal-clear waters, or simply relax in the sun. The gentle sway of the boat, the sound of the waves, and the beauty of the surroundings create a perfect setting for a day of romance and adventure.

Elephant Sanctuaries:

- **Ethical Interactions and Shared Experiences:** Visiting an ethical elephant sanctuary is a meaningful and memorable experience for couples who love animals. These sanctuaries provide a safe haven for elephants rescued from harsh conditions, and visitors can learn about elephant conservation while participating in activities such as feeding, bathing, and walking with the elephants.

Sharing this compassionate experience with your partner allows you to connect with each other and with these majestic creatures responsibly and ethically.

Romantic Dining Experiences

Dining in Thailand can be a deeply romantic experience, especially when you choose settings and experiences that offer privacy and intimacy.

Private Beach Dinners:

- **Customized Setups and Personal Chefs:** Imagine dining with your toes in the sand, the sound of the ocean as your soundtrack, and the stars twinkling above. Many luxury resorts in Thailand offer private beach dinners, where you can enjoy a gourmet meal prepared by a personal chef. The setup is often customized to your preferences, with options such as candlelit pathways, floral arrangements, and personalized menus. This exclusive dining experience is perfect for a special occasion or simply to create an unforgettable evening with your loved one.

Tree-house Dining (Soneva Kiri):

- **Elevated Dining with Stunning Views:** For a dining experience that literally takes romance to new heights, consider tree-house dining at Soneva Kiri on Koh Kood. Here, you'll be seated in a private tree pod high above the ground, with stunning rainforest and ocean views. Your meal, crafted from the finest local ingredients, is delivered by a personal waiter via zip line. The combination of exquisite food, breathtaking views, and the unique setting creates a dining experience that is as adventurous as it is romantic.

Tree House Dining

Floating Breakfast:

- **In-Villa Pools and Luxurious Spreads:** Start your day with a floating breakfast served in the privacy of your villa's pool. This luxurious experience involves a beautifully arranged breakfast spread, complete with fresh fruits, pastries, and your choice of beverages, all served on a floating tray. As you enjoy your meal while lounging in the pool, you can enjoy the tranquil surroundings and spend a leisurely morning with your partner. It's a unique and indulgent way to begin a day of relaxation or adventure.

River Cruises:

- **Dining on the Chao Phraya River with Live Music:** Experience the charm of Bangkok from a different perspective with a romantic dinner cruise on the Chao Phraya River. Gliding past iconic landmarks like Wat Arun and the Grand Palace, you'll be treated to a multi-course meal, live music, and the city's glittering lights. Many river cruises offer private seating options for couples, ensuring a more intimate experience as you dine and enjoy the views. The gentle rhythm of the river and the ambiance of the evening make this a memorable and romantic night out.

Cultural Experiences for Couples

Thailand's rich cultural heritage provides ample opportunities for couples to engage in meaningful and immersive experiences together.

Traditional Dance Performances:

- **Lanna Culture in Chiang Mai:** Attend a traditional Lanna dance performance in Chiang Mai to experience the grace and beauty of Northern Thailand's cultural heritage. These performances often occur in historic settings such as temples or cultural centers, including a traditional Northern Thai cuisine dinner. The intricate costumes, elegant movements, and haunting music create a captivating atmosphere that you can share with your partner.

Temple Visits:

- **Wat Phra That Doi Suthep and Sunset Prayers:** Visiting temples together can be a peaceful and spiritual experience for couples. Wat Phra That Doi Suthep, located on a mountain overlooking Chiang Mai, is one of Thailand's most revered temples. Arriving at sunset allows you to witness the golden stupa bathed in the evening light, followed by the sound of monks chanting during evening prayers. The tranquil ambiance and stunning views provide a serene setting for reflection and connection.

Local Festivals:

- **Participating in Loy Krathong and Releasing Lanterns Together:** Experience the magic of Thailand's festivals by participating in Loy Krathong, the Festival of Lights. During this festival, couples can create and release krathongs (floating baskets) into rivers or lakes, symbolizing the release of negativity and the beginning of a new chapter together. In Northern Thailand, you can also release sky lanterns into the night sky during Yi Peng, a parallel festival. These shared rituals are deeply symbolic and offer a unique way to celebrate your bond.

Craft Workshops:

- **Pottery and Traditional Weaving:** Engage in a creative activity together by joining a craft workshop. Learn traditional Thai pottery techniques or try weaving with local artisans. These workshops provide a fun and educational experience and a chance to take home a meaningful souvenir you've created together. The hands-on nature of these activities fosters collaboration and communication, deepening your connection as a couple.

Tips for Planning and Personalizing Romantic Activities

To make your romantic activities in Thailand truly special, consider these tips for planning and personalizing your experiences.

Customizing Experiences:

- **Adding Personal Touches and Special Requests:** Many romantic activities in Thailand can be customized to your preferences. Whether you'd like to arrange for a specific song to be played during your private dinner, choose your partner's favorite flowers for a surprise bouquet, or plan a proposal, don't hesitate to communicate your wishes to the service providers. Adding personal touches can make the experience even more memorable.

Booking in Advance:

- **Ensuring Availability and Avoiding Disappointment:** To secure the best experiences and avoid disappointment, it's advisable to book popular activities well in advance. This is especially important during peak travel seasons or for activities that have limited availability, such as hot air balloon rides or exclusive dining experiences. Early booking also allows you to have more flexibility in choosing the best times and dates.

Capturing Memories:

- **Hiring Photographers and Creating Keepsakes:** Consider hiring a professional photographer to capture your romantic moments, whether it's during a special activity like a hot air balloon ride or a private beach dinner. These photos can serve as beautiful keepsakes of your time together in Thailand. Additionally, creating a scrapbook or a digital album of your trip can help you preserve and relive the memories long after your return home.

Balancing Activities:

- **Mixing Relaxation with Adventure:** While filling your itinerary with exciting activities is tempting, balancing adventure and relaxation is essential. Include downtime for unwinding at the beach, enjoying a spa day, or simply relaxing by the pool. This balance ensures you return from your trip feeling rejuvenated and closer than ever.

Thailand offers countless opportunities for couples to create unique and romantic memories together. From the thrill of a sunrise hot air balloon ride over Chiang Mai to the serenity of a candlelit dinner on a secluded beach, the experiences outlined in this chapter are designed to foster connection, adventure, and intimacy. By thoughtfully planning and personalizing these activities, you can ensure that your romantic getaway in Thailand is filled with unforgettable moments that you and your partner will cherish for years to come.

CHAPTER 12: FAMILY-FRIENDLY ACTIVITIES

Family-Friendly Activities

Bangkok, Thailand's bustling capital, is not just a haven for culture enthusiasts and shoppers—it's also a fantastic destination for families with children. The city offers a variety of attractions and activities that cater to all ages, making it an ideal place for a family vacation. This chapter explores some of the best child-friendly attractions in Bangkok and other popular cities, from interactive museums and outdoor parks to entertainment complexes and family-friendly dining options. Whether you're looking for educational experiences or just some fun in the sun, Bangkok has something to keep every family member entertained.

Child-Friendly Attractions in Bangkok

Bangkok is home to several museums and attractions explicitly designed for children. These venues offer a mix of interactive exhibits, educational content, and hands-on activities that will keep young minds engaged and entertained.

Children's Discovery Museum:

- **Hands-On Exhibits, Science, and Learning:** Located in Chatuchak, the Children's Discovery Museum is a must-visit for families with curious kids. The museum features interactive exhibits that cover a wide range of topics, from science and technology to arts and culture. Children can engage in hands-on activities such as building robots, exploring a mock archaeological dig, or creating their art projects. The museum's playful and educational environment makes learning fun for kids of all ages.

Museum of Siam:

- **Interactive History Exhibits, Engaging Activities:** The Museum of Siam offers an interactive approach to learning about Thailand's rich history and culture. Children can explore the country's past through engaging exhibits, from ancient civilizations to modern-day Thailand. The museum's interactive displays, multimedia presentations, and hands-on activities make it an enjoyable and educational experience for both kids and adults.

Bangkok Art and Culture Centre:

- **Art Workshops, Family Programs:** The Bangkok Art and Culture Centre (BACC) is a hub for contemporary art and culture in the city. In addition to its rotating exhibitions, the BACC offers art workshops and family programs that encourage creativity and artistic expres-

CHAPTER 12: FAMILY-FRIENDLY ACTIVITIES

sion. These activities are designed to be accessible to children, making it a great place for families to explore art together.

SEA LIFE Bangkok Ocean World:

- **Marine Life Exhibits, Interactive Displays:** Located beneath the Siam Paragon shopping mall, SEA LIFE Bangkok Ocean World is one of Southeast Asia's largest aquariums. The aquarium is home to diverse marine life, including sharks, rays, penguins, and exotic fish. Interactive displays, such as the glass-bottom boat ride and touch pools, allow children to get up close and personal with the underwater world. The aquarium's immersive environments and educational exhibits make it a family hit.

Outdoor Parks and Playgrounds

Bangkok's green spaces offer a welcome respite from the city's hustle and bustle, and there is plenty of room for children to play and explore. Here are some of the best parks and playgrounds in the city.

Lumpini Park:

- **Playground, Paddle Boats, Outdoor Activities:** Lumpini Park, often referred to as the "green lung" of Bangkok, is a sprawling urban park that offers a variety of activities for families. Children can enjoy the well-maintained playgrounds, ride paddle boats on the park's lake, or watch the local monitor lizards that roam the area. The park also hosts outdoor fitness classes and cultural events, making it a vibrant community space.

Lumpini Park

CHAPTER 12: FAMILY-FRIENDLY ACTIVITIES

Benjakitti Park:

- **Biking Paths, Lake Views, and Play Areas:** Benjakitti Park, located near the Asok district, is another excellent spot for families. The park features scenic biking paths around a large lake and dedicated play areas for children. Families can rent bicycles or stroll around while enjoying the beautiful views of the Bangkok skyline. The park's tranquil atmosphere and well-maintained facilities make it a favorite among locals and tourists alike.

Chatuchak Park:

- **Children's Playground, Outdoor Fitness Areas:** Adjacent to the famous Chatuchak Weekend Market, Chatuchak Park offers a peaceful retreat with plenty of green space. The park's playground has swings, slides, and climbing frames, providing hours of entertainment for younger children. Additionally, the park has outdoor fitness areas where older kids and parents can stay active. After a day of shopping at the market, the park is the perfect place to relax and unwind.

Dusit Zoo:

- **Animal Exhibits, Petting Zoo:** Dusit Zoo, located near the Royal Palace, is one of Bangkok's oldest and most beloved attractions. The zoo is home to various animals, including elephants, giraffes, and tigers. In addition to the animal exhibits, there's a petting zoo where children can interact with gentler animals, such as goats and rabbits. The zoo also features a lake with paddle boats, playgrounds, and picnic areas, making it a full day of fun for the whole family.

Entertainment Complexes and Themed Attractions

For families seeking excitement and adventure, Bangkok offers several entertainment complexes and themed attractions that delight children of all ages.

Dream World:

- **Amusement Park Rides, Themed Zones:** Dream World is Bangkok's answer to a classic amusement park, complete with thrilling rides, themed zones, and live shows. The park is divided into themed areas, including Fantasy Land, Adventure Land, and Snow Town, where children can play in artificial snow. With a wide range of attractions—from gentle rides for toddlers to adrenaline-pumping roller coasters—Dream World offers something for everyone.

CHAPTER 12: FAMILY-FRIENDLY ACTIVITIES

Dream World Entrance

KidZania Bangkok:

- **Interactive Role-Playing, Educational Fun:** Located in the Siam Paragon shopping mall, KidZania Bangkok is an indoor "edutainment" center where children can explore different careers through interactive role-playing activities. Kids can try to be pilots, doctors, firefighters, or chefs in a safe, controlled environment. The realistic settings and engaging scenarios make learning fun, and parents can relax in the lounge area while their children play.

Safari World:

- **Animal Shows, Safari Park:** Safari World is a large wildlife park that offers a unique blend of safari adventures and animal shows. Families can drive close to the open-air safari park to see animals such as zebras, giraffes, and lions. The park also features a marine park with live shows, including a dolphin show, a sea lion performance, and an entertaining stunt show. Safari World's combination of education and entertainment makes it a popular destination for family outings.

Siam Park City:

- **Water Park, Amusement Rides:** Siam Park City is both an amusement park and a water park, making it a perfect destination for a full day of fun. The park's water attractions include a giant wave pool, water slides, and a lazy river, while the amusement park offers a variety of rides, from gentle carousels to thrilling roller coasters. Siam Park City is an excellent choice for families looking to cool off and enjoy some excitement in the heart of Bangkok.

Family-Friendly Dining in Bangkok

Finding a restaurant catering to adults and children is easy in Bangkok. There are plenty of dining options that offer kid-friendly menus and entertainment.

CHAPTER 12: FAMILY-FRIENDLY ACTIVITIES

Caturday Cat Cafe:

- **Pet-Friendly, Cat Interactions:** Located near BTS Ratchathewi, Caturday Cat Cafe is a delightful spot for families who love animals. The cafe is home to various friendly cats that children can pet and play with while enjoying a meal or a snack. The menu includes a range of comfort foods, desserts, and beverages, making it a fun and relaxing place for both kids and parents.

Kuppa:

- **Kid-Friendly Menu, Play Area:** Kuppa is a family-friendly restaurant located in the Sukhumvit area. The restaurant offers a diverse menu with plenty of options for children, including pasta, burgers, and healthy snacks. Kuppa also features a dedicated play area where children can entertain themselves while parents enjoy a leisurely meal. The warm and welcoming atmosphere makes it a great choice for family dining.

The Commons:

- **Community Mall, Play Spaces, Diverse Dining Options:** The Commons, located in Thonglor, has many dining options and play spaces for children. The open-air market space is home to various food vendors, offering everything from Thai street food to international cuisine. Families can enjoy their meals in a relaxed, communal setting while children explore the dedicated play areas. The Commons also hosts family-friendly events and workshops, making it a vibrant and lively spot for a family outing.

Chocolate Ville:

- **Themed Dining, Outdoor Seating, Scenic Views:** Chocolate Ville is a themed dining park located on the outskirts of Bangkok. The park is designed to resemble a European village, complete with charming buildings, a river, and bridges. The outdoor seating areas offer scenic views, and the menu features a wide range of dishes that cater to all tastes. The picturesque setting and family-friendly atmosphere make Chocolate Ville popular for a special family meal.

Bangkok is a city that truly caters to families, offering a wealth of attractions, activities, and dining options that will entertain both children and adults. From interactive museums and exciting amusement parks to green spaces and family-friendly restaurants, there's no shortage of things to do with your little ones in the bustling capital. By exploring the recommendations in this chapter, you can create a fun and memorable family vacation in Bangkok filled with learning, adventure, and plenty of smiles.

Family Adventures in Chiang Mai

Chiang Mai, the cultural heart of Northern Thailand, is an ideal destination for families seeking adventure, education, and immersion in nature. Known for its rich history, vibrant arts scene, and stunning natural landscapes, Chiang Mai offers various activities for children and adults. In this section, we'll explore some of the best family-friendly experiences in Chiang Mai, from nature and wildlife encounters to cultural workshops, outdoor adventures, and family-friendly accommodations. Whether you're traveling with young children or teenagers, Chiang Mai has something to offer every family.

Nature and Wildlife Experiences

Chiang Mai's lush landscapes and abundant wildlife provide endless opportunities for families to connect with nature and learn about the region's unique ecosystems.

Elephant Nature Park:

- **Ethical Elephant Interactions and Family Tours:** Located about an hour outside of Chiang Mai, Elephant Nature Park is a sanctuary and rescue center for elephants. Unlike traditional elephant camps, this park focuses on providing a safe and natural environment for its elephants, many of which have been rescued from complex lives in logging or tourism. Families can participate in day tours where they learn about elephant care, feed the elephants, and observe them in their natural habitat. The experience is both educational and heartwarming, making it a must-do for families who want to engage in responsible tourism.

Elephant Nature Park

CHAPTER 12: FAMILY-FRIENDLY ACTIVITIES

Chiang Mai Night Safari:

- **Nocturnal Animal Encounters and Tram Rides:** The Chiang Mai Night Safari offers a unique opportunity to see active animals after dark. The park is divided into several zones, each featuring different wildlife species, from large predators to gentle herbivores. Families can explore the park on foot or take a tram ride through the various zones, where they'll see animals like lions, tigers, and giraffes. The tram rides are accompanied by informative guides who share interesting facts about the animals. The night safari is an exciting and educational experience that's sure to be a hit with children of all ages.

Queen Sirikit Botanic Garden:

- **Plant Collections and Canopy Walkway:** Nestled in the mountains just outside of Chiang Mai, the Queen Sirikit Botanic Garden is a beautiful place to spend a day with the family. The garden is home to an impressive collection of plants worldwide, including tropical rainforest species, orchids, and medicinal plants. One of the garden's highlights is the canopy walkway, a series of elevated paths that offer stunning views of the surrounding forest. Families can also explore the various greenhouses, stroll through the themed gardens, or picnic in the scenic surroundings.

Queen Sirikit Canopy Walk

Huay Tung Tao Lake:

- **Swimming, Paddle Boating, and Picnicking:** Huay Tung Tao Lake is popular with locals and tourists and is about 20 minutes from Chiang Mai City. Mountains surround the lake and offer a peaceful retreat from the city. Families can enjoy swimming, paddle boating, or simply relaxing by the water. There are also bamboo huts along the shore where you can order food and have a picnic. The lake's calm and shallow waters make it a safe place for children to swim, and the surrounding area is perfect for a family day out in nature.

Cultural and Creative Workshops

Chiang Mai is renowned for its rich cultural heritage, and there are plenty of opportunities for families to engage in creative and educational activities together.

Art in Paradise:

- **3D Art Museum and Interactive Exhibits:** Art in Paradise is an interactive 3D art museum where visitors can become part of the artwork. The museum features large-scale paintings that create optical illusions, allowing visitors to pose in ways that make it look like they're part of the scene. Kids and adults alike will have a blast taking photos and exploring the different themed rooms, from underwater worlds to ancient ruins. It's a fun and creative way to spend an afternoon; your photos will make great memories.

Thai Cooking Classes:

- **Family-Friendly, Hands-On Cooking Experiences:** Chiang Mai is famous for its cuisine, and taking a family cooking class is a fantastic way to learn more about Thai food. Many cooking schools in Chiang Mai offer family-friendly classes where children can participate in the cooking process. Classes typically include visiting a local market to pick out fresh ingredients, followed by a hands-on cooking session where you'll learn to prepare classic Thai dishes like pad Thai, green curry, and mango sticky rice. Sitting down to enjoy the delicious meal you've created together is the best part.

Thai Cooking Class

Traditional Thai Dance Classes:

- **Cultural Immersion and Fun Learning:** For a unique cultural experience, consider enrolling your family in a traditional Thai dance class. These classes are designed to introduce participants to Thai classical dance's graceful movements and intricate costumes. Instructors will guide you through the basic steps and explain the significance of the dance in Thai culture. It's a fun and interactive way for children to learn about Thailand's artistic traditions while getting some exercise at the same time.

Traditional Thai Dancing

Craft Workshops:

- **Umbrella Painting and Pottery Making:** Chiang Mai is known for its traditional crafts, and many local artisans offer workshops where families can learn these skills together. One popular option is umbrella painting in the village of Bo Sang, where you can paint your own parasol using traditional techniques. Another option is pottery making, where you'll learn to shape and decorate your clay creations. These workshops are hands-on and engaging, and you'll have a beautiful handmade souvenir to take home as a reminder of your time in Chiang Mai.

Umbrella Painting

Outdoor Adventure Activities

For families who love the outdoors, Chiang Mai offers plenty of adventure activities that are suitable for all ages.

CHAPTER 12: FAMILY-FRIENDLY ACTIVITIES

Zip-Lining:

- **Flight of the Gibbon and Family-Friendly Courses:** Zip-lining is one of the most popular adventure activities in Chiang Mai, and several operators cater to families. Flight of the Gibbon is one of the most well-known zip-lining companies in the area, offering a course that takes you through the rainforest treetops. The course is designed to be safe and accessible for children, with experienced guides ensuring everyone is secure and comfortable. Zip-lining offers a thrilling way to experience the beauty of the forest from a unique perspective.

Cycling Tours:

- **Scenic Routes and Rural Landscapes:** Exploring the countryside around Chiang Mai by bicycle is an excellent way for families to enjoy the outdoors and experience the local way of life. Several cycling tour operators offer family-friendly routes, ranging from gentle rides through rice paddies and small villages to more challenging mountain routes. Many tours include stops at local farms, temples, and markets, providing plenty of opportunities for rest and exploration.

Hiking:

- **Doi Suthep and Family-Friendly Trails:** Chiang Mai is surrounded by mountains and forests, making it an excellent destination for hiking. One of the most popular hikes is up Doi Suthep, the mountain that overlooks the city. The hike takes you through the lush forest to the Wat Phra That Doi Suthep temple, where you'll be rewarded with stunning views of Chiang Mai. For families with younger children, there are also shorter, easier trails in the area that offer beautiful scenery without the need for strenuous effort.

Hot Air Balloon Rides:

- **Scenic Views and Family Packages:** For a truly unforgettable experience, consider taking your family on a hot air balloon ride over the Chiang Mai countryside. The early morning flight offers breathtaking views of the mountains, forests, and rice fields as the sun rises. Many companies offer family packages that include a post-flight breakfast and a certificate of completion. It's a peaceful and awe-inspiring way to see the landscape from a new perspective and one that your family will remember for years to come.

Family-Friendly Accommodations in Chiang Mai

Having suitable accommodations can make all the difference when traveling with children. Chiang Mai offers a wide range of family-friendly hotels and guesthouses that cater to the needs of families.

CHAPTER 12: FAMILY-FRIENDLY ACTIVITIES

Family Suites:

- **Spacious Rooms and Kid-Friendly Amenities:** Many hotels in Chiang Mai offer family suites that provide extra space and amenities designed for families. These suites often include separate sleeping areas for parents and children and kitchenettes or dining areas. Look for hotels that offer kid-friendly amenities such as cribs, high chairs, and toys, ensuring a comfortable stay for the whole family.

Pool Facilities:

- **Child-Safe Swimming Pools:** After a day of exploring Chiang Mai, kids will love cooling off in the hotel pool. Many family-friendly hotels in the city offer pools with shallow areas or separate kiddie pools that are safe for children. Some hotels also have poolside snacks and drinks available, making it easy for parents to relax while the kids play.

On-Site Activities:

- **Kids' Clubs and Play Areas:** Some hotels and resorts in Chiang Mai offer on-site activities specifically for children, such as kids' clubs, play areas, and organized games. These activities provide children entertainment and allow parents to relax or enjoy some adult-only time. Check with your hotel to see what on-site activities are available and plan your stay accordingly.

Babysitting Services:

- **Reliable and Experienced Caregivers:** Many hotels in Chiang Mai offer babysitting services for parents who want to enjoy a night out or a day of solo exploration. These services are provided by reliable and experienced caregivers who can look after your children in the comfort of your hotel room. Please be sure to ask about babysitting options when booking your accommodation and make arrangements in advance if you need them.

Chiang Mai is a destination that offers endless opportunities for family adventures, from exploring nature and wildlife to engaging in cultural workshops and outdoor activities. The city's family-friendly atmosphere, rich cultural heritage, and stunning natural beauty make it an ideal place for a memorable family vacation. By following the recommendations in this chapter, you can ensure that your family's time in Chiang Mai is filled with fun, learning, and unforgettable experiences that will bring you closer together.

Beach Activities for Kids in Phuket

Phuket, Thailand's largest island, is famous for its beautiful beaches and crystal-clear waters, making it an ideal destination for families seeking sun, sand, and sea. With its wide range of kid-friendly activities, family-oriented resorts, and nearby attractions, Phuket offers everything you need for a fun-filled beach vacation. In this section, we'll explore some of the best beach activities for children, recommend family-friendly resorts, highlight nearby attractions, and provide essential tips for ensuring a safe and enjoyable beach experience for the whole family.

Water-Based Activities for Children

Phuket's calm, warm waters and extensive shoreline make it perfect for various water-based activities that kids will love. Here are some of the top fun and safe activities for children.

Snorkeling:

- **Shallow Reefs and Calm Waters:** Phuket offers several beaches with shallow reefs close to the shore, making snorkeling a safe and enjoyable activity for kids. Beaches like Kata Noi and Nai Harn have calm waters that are perfect for beginners. Children can explore the vibrant underwater world, spotting colorful fish and coral without needing to venture too far from the shore. It's a great way to introduce kids to marine life and the joys of snorkeling in a safe environment.

Kayaking:

- **Family-Friendly Tours and Guided Trips:** Kayaking is a fantastic way for families to explore Phuket's coastline and nearby islands. Many beaches and resorts offer kayak rentals or guided tours suitable for families with children. Beaches like Ao Sane and Laem Singh are great starting points for kayaking adventures, where kids can paddle along the shoreline, explore hidden coves, and enjoy the stunning scenery. Double kayaks allow parents to paddle with younger children for safety and fun.

Banana Boat Rides:

- **Safe and Thrilling Experience:** For a bit of excitement, try a banana boat ride—a popular beach activity where kids (and adults) can enjoy the thrill of being towed behind a speedboat on an inflatable banana-shaped raft. The ride is fast, fun, and usually accompanied by plenty of laughter as the boat weaves through the water, creating waves and splashes. Life jackets are provided, and the rides are supervised by experienced operators, ensuring a safe yet exhilarating experience for kids.

Banana Boat Ride

CHAPTER 12: FAMILY-FRIENDLY ACTIVITIES

Beach Games:

- **Volleyball and Sandcastle Building:** Sometimes, the simplest activities are the most enjoyable. Phuket's beaches provide the perfect setting for classic beach games like volleyball, Frisbee, or soccer. Many beaches have volleyball nets set up, and it's easy to join in or start a game with other beachgoers. Building sandcastles is a timeless beach activity for younger kids that can keep them entertained for hours. Phuket's soft, fine sand is perfect for creating elaborate sand structures; parents can join in the fun too.

Family-Friendly Beach Resorts

Phuket is home to numerous resorts that cater specifically to families. These resorts offer amenities and activities designed to keep children entertained and parents relaxed. Here are some of the top family-friendly beach resorts in Phuket.

JW Marriott Phuket Resort & Spa:

- **Kid's Club and Family Pools:** Located on Mai Khao Beach, JW Marriott Phuket Resort & Spa is a luxurious resort that offers a range of amenities for families. The resort features a dedicated kid's club with daily activities, a playground, and multiple family-friendly pools. A children's pavilion with a kids' menu and fun dining experiences is also available. The resort's spacious rooms and suites can accommodate families of all sizes, making it an excellent choice for a beach vacation.

Katathani Phuket Beach Resort:

- **Children's Pool and Playground:** Katathani Phuket Beach Resort, located on Kata Noi Beach, is another great family option. The resort offers a dedicated children's pool, a fun playground, and a variety of family-oriented activities. The beachfront location means you're just steps away from the sand, and the resort's restaurants offer kid-friendly menus. The resort's quiet, laid-back atmosphere makes it ideal for families looking for a relaxing getaway.

Katathani Phuket Beach Resort

CHAPTER 12: FAMILY-FRIENDLY ACTIVITIES

Centara Grand Beach Resort:

- **Water Park and Kids' Activities:** Situated on Karon Beach, Centara Grand Beach Resort is a family favorite, thanks to its on-site water park, which features water slides, a lazy river, and a dedicated kids' pool. The resort also offers a range of kids' activities, from arts and crafts to treasure hunts, ensuring that there's never a dull moment. The spacious family suites provide plenty of room, and the resort's restaurants offer both Thai and international cuisine with options for children.

Sunwing Kamala Beach:

- **Family Suites and Entertainment Programs:** Sunwing Kamala Beach is designed with families in mind, offering family suites equipped with kitchenettes, baby cots, and bunk beds. The resort's entertainment programs include everything from kids' shows to pool games, and there's even a dedicated mascot who interacts with the children. The resort's location on Kamala Beach provides easy access to the sand and sea, and the surrounding area offers plenty of dining and shopping options.

Sunwing Kamala Beach Resort

Nearby Attractions and Excursions

In addition to beach activities, Phuket offers a variety of nearby attractions and excursions that are perfect for family outings.

Phuket Aquarium:

- **Marine Life Exhibits and Interactive Tanks:** Located at the southern tip of Cape Panwa, Phuket Aquarium is a small but well-curated facility showcasing the Andaman Sea's marine life. Kids will love the colorful displays of tropical fish, sea turtles, and other marine creatures.

The aquarium also features interactive touch tanks where children can safely explore marine life up close. It's an educational and entertaining outing that's perfect for a break from the beach.

Dino Park Mini Golf:

- **Dinosaur-Themed Mini-Golf, Fun for All Ages:** Dino Park Mini Golf, located between Kata and Karon beaches, is a family-friendly attraction that combines mini-golf with a prehistoric theme. The course is set among life-sized dinosaur statues, volcanic caves, and waterfalls, creating an exciting and immersive experience for kids. After a round of mini-golf, families can enjoy a meal at the on-site restaurant, which is also dinosaur-themed.

EXPLORE THAILAND: A COMPREHENSIVE TRAVEL GUIDE FOR FIRST-TIMERS

CHAPTER 12: FAMILY-FRIENDLY ACTIVITIES

Phuket Trick-eye Museum:

- **3D Art and Interactive Photo Ops:** The Phuket Trick-eye Museum in Phuket Town is an interactive 3D art museum where kids can become part of the exhibits. The museum features a variety of large-scale paintings that create optical illusions, allowing visitors to pose in ways that make it look like they're part of the scene. It's a fun and creative way to spend an afternoon, and the resulting photos will surely be a hit with friends and family.

Phuket FantaSea:

- **Cultural Theme Park and Family Shows:** Phuket FantaSea is a cultural theme park that offers a blend of entertainment, dining, and Thai cultural experiences. The park's main attraction is its evening show, which features acrobatics, live animals, and traditional Thai performances in a spectacular display of lights and sound. There's also a carnival village with games, shopping, and a buffet dinner, making it a full evening of entertainment for the whole family.

Viva Bangkok Stage at Phuket FantaSea

Tips for Beach Safety and Comfort

Consider these practical tips to ensure that your family's beach experience in Phuket is safe and enjoyable.

Sun Protection:

- **Sunscreen, Hats, and Beach Tents:** Phuket's tropical sun can be intense, especially for young children. Be sure to apply sunscreen regularly, wear hats, and consider bringing a beach tent or umbrella to provide shade. Long-sleeve swimwear with UV protection is also a good option for keeping kids safe from the sun.

Hydration:

- **Bringing Plenty of Water and** Beachside Cafes: Staying hydrated is crucial when spending time on the beach. Pack plenty of water for your family, or take advantage of the many beachside cafes where you can grab a refreshing drink. Be mindful of the heat and encourage children to take breaks in the shade to avoid overheating.

Supervision:

- **Keeping an Eye on Children and Lifeguard Presence:** Always closely watch your children while they're playing in the water or on the beach. Many of Phuket's popular beaches have lifeguards on duty, but it's still important to remain vigilant. Ensure your children understand basic water safety rules, such as staying within a certain distance from the shore.

First Aid:

- **Basic Supplies and Knowing Nearby Medical Facilities:** Accidents can happen, so it's a good idea to bring a small first aid kit with essentials like band-aids, antiseptic wipes, and pain relievers. Familiarize yourself with the location of nearby medical facilities or pharmacies, just in case you need assistance during your trip.

Phuket is a paradise for families, offering a perfect blend of beach activities, family-friendly resorts, and exciting attractions that cater to children of all ages. Whether your kids are exploring the underwater world through snorkeling, enjoying a thrilling banana boat ride, or getting creative at the Trickeye Museum, there's no shortage of fun. By following the recommendations and tips in this chapter, you can ensure a safe, comfortable, and unforgettable beach vacation for your family in Phuket.

CHAPTER 13: ECO-TOURISM & SUSTAINABILITY

Eco-Tourism and Sustainability

As travelers become increasingly aware of their journeys' environmental impact, Eco-tourism and sustainable travel practices are becoming more critical. With its rich biodiversity and natural beauty, Thailand is a prime destination for Eco-conscious travelers. Whether you're staying in a jungle lodge, a beachfront bungalow, or a luxury resort, numerous Eco-friendly accommodations allow you to experience the best of Thailand while minimizing your environmental footprint. In this chapter, we'll explore what makes an accommodation Eco-friendly, highlight some of Thailand's top Eco-friendly resorts and lodges, discuss the benefits of sustainable travel, and provide tips for identifying and booking Eco-friendly stays. We will also discuss responsible animal tourism and supporting local communities to achieve maximum sustainability within Thailand.

Eco-Friendly Accommodations

Eco-friendly accommodations are designed and operated to minimize environmental impact and promote sustainability. These accommodations often incorporate a range of practices aimed at conserving natural resources, reducing waste, and supporting local communities.

Sustainable Building Materials:

- **Bamboo and Recycled Materials:** One of the critical aspects of Eco-friendly accommodations is the use of sustainable building materials. Bamboo, a rapidly renewable resource, is often used in construction because of its strength, flexibility, and low environmental impact. Recycled materials, such as reclaimed wood or repurposed metal, are also commonly used to reduce the need for new resources and minimize waste.

Energy-Efficient Systems:

- **Solar Panels and Wind Turbines:** Eco-friendly accommodations often use renewable energy sources, such as solar panels or wind turbines, to power their operations. These systems reduce reliance on fossil fuels and decrease greenhouse gas emissions. Energy-efficient lighting, heating, cooling systems, natural ventilation, and insulation further reduce the accommodation's carbon footprint.

CHAPTER 13: ECO-TOURISM & SUSTAINABILITY

Water Conservation:

- **Rainwater Harvesting and Low-Flow Fixtures:** Water conservation is critical to Eco-friendly accommodations. Rainwater harvesting systems collect and store rainwater for irrigation, laundry, and other non-potable applications. Low-flow fixtures like shower heads and toilets reduce water consumption without sacrificing comfort. Additionally, many Eco-friendly accommodations use native plants in their landscaping to minimize the need for irrigation.

Waste Management:

- **Composting and Recycling Programs:** Effective waste management practices are essential for minimizing the environmental impact of accommodations. Composting programs turn organic waste into nutrient-rich compost for use in gardens and landscaping, while recycling programs ensure that materials like paper, glass, and plastics are appropriately processed. Some accommodations even have policies to reduce single-use plastics by providing refillable water bottles and eliminating plastic straws.

Top Eco-Friendly Resorts and Lodges in Thailand

Thailand is home to several Eco-friendly resorts and lodges that are leading the way in sustainable tourism. These accommodations combine luxury and comfort with a commitment to environmental stewardship.

Anantara Golden Triangle Elephant Camp & Resort:

- **Conservation Programs and Low-Impact Tourism:** Located in the lush mountains of northern Thailand, the Anantara Golden Triangle Elephant Camp & Resort is known for its commitment to wildlife conservation and sustainable tourism. The resort is deeply involved in elephant conservation efforts, offering guests the chance to learn about and interact with elephants ethically and responsibly. The resort's design incorporates sustainable building materials, and its operations focus on minimizing waste and energy use. Guests can enjoy luxury accommodations while knowing that their stay supports important conservation work.

Anantara Golden Triangle Elephant Camp & Resort

CHAPTER 13: ECO-TOURISM & SUSTAINABILITY

Soneva Kiri (Koh Kood):

- **Eco-Luxury and Renewable Energy:** Soneva Kiri, located on the unspoiled island of Koh Kood, offers a blend of luxury and sustainability. The resort's villas are designed to blend seamlessly with the natural environment, using locally sourced materials and sustainable construction methods. Soneva Kiri is powered by renewable energy, including solar and wind, and firmly commits to reducing waste and conserving water. The resort also operates an organic garden that supplies fresh produce for its restaurants, ensuring that guests enjoy healthy, locally sourced meals.

The Tongsai Bay (Koh Samui):

- **Zero-Waste Policy and Natural Surroundings:** The Tongsai Bay on Koh Samui is a pioneer in Eco-friendly hospitality, having implemented a zero-waste policy that aims to reduce waste to the absolute minimum. The resort's buildings are constructed from sustainable materials and are designed to harmonize with the natural landscape. Guests are encouraged to explore the resort's lush gardens and beachfront, where native plants and wildlife thrive. The Tongsai Bay's commitment to sustainability extends to its dining options, which feature organic, locally sourced ingredients.

Keemala (Phuket):

- **Organic Gardens and Sustainable Architecture:** Keemala, located in the hills of Phuket, offers a unique and luxurious Eco-friendly experience. The resort's villas are inspired by traditional Thai architecture and are built using sustainable materials. Keemala's organic gardens provide fresh produce for its restaurants, and the resort is committed to minimizing its environmental impact through water conservation, waste reduction, and energy efficiency. Guests can enjoy spa treatments, wellness programs, and outdoor activities while harmonizing with nature.

Benefits of Staying in Eco-Friendly Accommodations

Choosing to stay in Eco-friendly accommodations offers a range of benefits, both for the environment and for your overall travel experience.

Environmental Impact:

- **Reducing Carbon Footprint:** Eco-friendly accommodations are designed to minimize their carbon footprint by using renewable energy, conserving water, and reducing waste. By staying in such accommodations, you're actively contributing to reducing greenhouse gas emissions and helping to protect the planet's natural resources.

Community Support:

- **Providing Local Employment and Supporting Local Businesses:** Many Eco-friendly accommodations prioritize hiring local staff and sourcing materials and products from nearby communities. This approach supports the local economy and helps preserve cultural traditions and crafts. Staying in Eco-friendly accommodations often means directly contributing to the local community's wellbeing.

Health Benefits:

- **Access to Organic Food and Natural Environments:** Eco-friendly accommodations often emphasize wellness and healthy living. This can include access to organic, locally grown food and opportunities to connect with nature through activities like hiking, gardening, or wildlife observation. These experiences can contribute to a sense of well-being and relaxation, making your stay more enjoyable and rejuvenating.

Educational Opportunities:

- **Learning About Sustainability and Eco-Tours:** Many Eco-friendly accommodations offer educational programs and tours that allow guests to learn about sustainability practices, local ecosystems, and conservation efforts. These experiences can deepen your understanding of the natural world and inspire you to adopt more sustainable habits in your everyday life.

Tips for Identifying and Booking Eco-Friendly Stays

Finding and booking Eco-friendly accommodations can enhance your travel experience while supporting sustainability. Here are some tips to help you choose the right place to stay.

Certification Labels:

- **Green Globe, Earth Check:** Look for certification labels indicating an accommodation's sustainability commitment. Organizations like Green Globe and Earth Check assess properties based on their environmental practices, social responsibility, and overall sustainability. These certifications provide assurance that the accommodation meets high standards for Eco-friendly operations.

Reading Reviews:

- **Online Platforms and Eco-Travel Blogs:** Read reviews from other travelers who have stayed at the accommodation before booking. Online platforms like Trip Advisor and Booking.com often include information on a property's sustainability practices. Additionally, Eco-travel blogs and websites can be valuable resources for finding recommendations and detailed reviews of Eco-friendly accommodations.

Direct Inquiries:

- **Contacting Accommodations About Their Practices:** If you're unsure about an accommodation's sustainability practices, don't hesitate to contact them directly. Ask questions about their energy use, waste management, water conservation efforts, and community involvement. Most Eco-friendly accommodations are proud of their practices and will gladly provide detailed information.

Comparing Options:

- **Balancing Cost and Sustainability:** While Eco-friendly accommodations can sometimes be more expensive, the benefits often justify the cost. Consider what's most important to you—reducing your environmental impact, supporting local communities, or enjoying a unique travel experience. Weigh these factors against the cost to find an accommodation that aligns with your values and budget.

Eco-tourism and sustainability are becoming increasingly crucial as travelers seek ways to minimize their environmental impact while exploring the world. By choosing to stay in Eco-friendly accommodations, you can enjoy a more meaningful and responsible travel experience, knowing that your stay contributes to preserving Thailand's natural beauty and cultural heritage. Whether you're seeking luxury in an Eco-resort or a more rustic experience in a jungle lodge, the options are plentiful and varied. Use the tips and recommendations in this chapter to find the perfect Eco-friendly accommodation for your next trip to Thailand, and take pride in knowing that your travel choices are making a positive difference.

Responsible Wildlife Tourism

As awareness of the impact of tourism on wildlife grows, responsible wildlife tourism has become an essential consideration for ethical travelers. Thailand, with its rich biodiversity and unique ecosystems, offers numerous opportunities to engage with wildlife in a way that supports conservation and protects animal welfare. This section will guide you through the principles of responsible wildlife tourism, highlight ethical wildlife experiences in Thailand, discuss the positive impact of responsible tourism, and provide practical tips for ensuring that your interactions with wildlife are both ethical and meaningful.

Principles of Responsible Wildlife Tourism

Responsible wildlife tourism is about ensuring that interactions with animals are conducted in a way that prioritizes their well-being and supports conservation efforts. Here are the key principles to keep in mind:

Avoiding Exploitation:

- **No Animal Performances or Elephant Riding:** One of the most important aspects of responsible wildlife tourism is avoiding activities that exploit animals for entertainment. This includes animal performances, where animals are often forced to perform unnatural behaviors, and elephant riding, which can cause significant physical and psychological harm to the animals. Instead, seek experiences that allow you to observe animals in their natural habitats or environments where their well-being is the top priority.

Supporting Sanctuaries:

- **Accredited, Non-Profit Organizations:** When choosing to visit a wildlife sanctuary, it is crucial to select accredited organizations that operate as non-profits. These sanctuaries should focus on rehabilitating and caring for animals rather than profit-driven tourism. Look for sanctuaries that prioritize animal welfare, provide transparent information about their practices, and are involved in conservation efforts.

Observing Wildlife:

- **From a Safe and Respectful Distance:** Ethical wildlife tourism emphasizes the importance of observing animals from a distance that does not disturb them. This ensures that animals can behave naturally without feeling threatened or stressed by human presence. Use binoculars or zoom lenses to get a closer look, and follow any guidelines provided by wildlife experts or guides.

Educating Oneself:

- **Learning About Local Wildlife and Conservation Efforts:** A key component of responsible wildlife tourism is educating yourself about the animals you're encountering and the conservation issues they face. This can include learning about the species' behaviors, habitats, and threats from poaching, habitat loss, or human-wildlife conflict. The more informed you are, the more you can contribute to their protection and conservation.

Ethical Wildlife Experiences in Thailand

Thailand offers several ethical wildlife experiences where visitors can engage with animals responsibly and respectfully. These organizations are dedicated to the welfare of the animals and the conservation of their habitats.

Elephant Nature Park (Chiang Mai):

- **Ethical Elephant Interactions and Volunteer Programs:** Elephant Nature Park is one of Thailand's most well-known ethical elephant sanctuaries. Located near Chiang Mai, this sanctuary is home to rescued elephants that have been saved from abusive conditions in the logging and tourism industries. Visitors can spend a day at the park to feed, observe, and learn about the elephants in a natural and safe environment. The park also offers volunteer programs, allowing participants to contribute to the care and well-being of the elephants.

Gibbon Rehabilitation Project (Phuket):

- **Gibbon Care and Forest Rehabilitation:** The Gibbon Rehabilitation Project (GRP) in Phuket is dedicated to rescuing and rehabilitating gibbons that have been ex-

CHAPTER 13: ECO-TOURISM & SUSTAINABILITY

ploited by the illegal pet trade and tourism industry. The project works to reintroduce these gibbons to the wild in a protected forest area. Visitors can learn about the plight of gibbons in Thailand, observe them in a semi-wild environment, and support the project's efforts through donations or volunteer work.

Gibbon Rehabilitation Facility

Phuket Elephant Sanctuary:

- **Retirement Home for Elephants and Visitor Education:** Phuket Elephant Sanctuary is a retirement home for elephants who have spent their lives in the logging and tourism industries. The sanctuary provides a peaceful environment where elephants can roam freely, socialize, and recover from years of hard labor. Visitors are invited to observe the elephants as they go about their daily lives, with no riding or direct contact allowed. The sanctuary emphasizes education, providing visitors with insights into the ethical treatment of elephants and the importance of conservation.

Marine Conservation Cambodia:

- **Coral Reef Restoration and Marine Life Protection:** While not located in Thailand, Marine Conservation Cambodia (MCC) offers valuable lessons in marine conservation that can inspire similar efforts in Thai waters. MCC focuses on protecting and restoring coral reefs, conserving marine life, and educating local communities about sustainable fishing practices. Visitors and volunteers can participate in coral planting, marine surveys, and beach clean-ups, contributing directly to preserving marine ecosystems.

The Impact of Responsible Wildlife Tourism

Responsible wildlife tourism has far-reaching benefits that extend beyond your individual experience. Here's how your ethical choices can make a positive impact:

CHAPTER 13: ECO-TOURISM & SUSTAINABILITY

Funding Conservation:

- **Entrance Fees Supporting Projects:** Many ethical wildlife experiences, such as visiting sanctuaries or participating in conservation programs, charge entrance fees that directly support the operation and expansion of conservation efforts. These funds are used to care for animals, protect habitats, and finance community outreach programs, ensuring that your visit has a lasting positive effect.

Raising Awareness:

- **Educating Visitors on Wildlife Issues:** Responsible wildlife tourism often includes educational components that help raise awareness about the challenges facing wildlife. By learning about issues like habitat destruction, poaching, and the illegal wildlife trade, visitors can become advocates for conservation, spreading the message and encouraging others to make ethical travel choices.

Enhancing Local Economies:

- **Providing Jobs and Supporting Local Communities:** Ethical wildlife tourism can provide valuable economic benefits to local communities. By creating jobs in conservation, education, and hospitality, these initiatives help support local economies while promoting sustainable practices. Additionally, many projects involve local communities in conservation efforts, ensuring that the benefits of tourism are shared and that traditional knowledge is integrated into modern conservation strategies.

Protecting Habitats:

- **Reducing Human-Wildlife Conflict and Preserving Ecosystems:** Responsible wildlife tourism helps protect natural habitats by reducing the need for harmful activities like deforestation, poaching, or illegal land use. By supporting sanctuaries and conservation projects, visitors contribute to preserving ecosystems, ensuring that wildlife has a safe and secure environment in which to thrive. This, in turn, reduces human-wildlife conflict and helps maintain the delicate balance of local ecosystems.

Tips for Ensuring Responsible Wildlife Interactions

To ensure that your wildlife encounters are ethical and respectful, consider these practical tips:

Researching Organizations:

- **Checking Credentials and Reading Reviews:** Before visiting any wildlife-related attraction, take the time to research the organization's credentials and read reviews from other travelers. Look for certifications from reputable conservation bodies and seek testimonials highlighting ethical practices. Avoid organizations that promote direct contact with wild animals or offer entertainment-focused experiences.

Avoiding Harmful Activities:

- **No Selfies with Sedated Animals or Direct Contact:** One of the fundamental principles of responsible wildlife tourism is to avoid activities that harm or exploit animals. This includes taking selfies with sedated animals, riding elephants, or engaging in any activity that involves direct contact with wild animals. Instead, focus on observing animals from a distance and learning about their natural behaviors.

Supporting Local Guides:

- **Hiring Knowledgeable and Ethical Guides:** When visiting wildlife areas or participating in nature tours, consider hiring local guides who are knowledgeable about the area's wildlife and conservation efforts. Ethical guides can enhance your experience by providing insights into animal behavior, ecosystem dynamics, and the importance of conservation. They can also ensure that your interactions with wildlife are conducted safely and respectfully.

Following Guidelines:

- **Respecting Rules and Regulations and Listening to Staff:** Always follow the guidelines and rules set by wildlife sanctuaries, conservation projects, and tour operators. These rules are in place to protect both the animals and the visitors. Please listen to the instructions of staff and guides, and respect their expertise in making sure that your experience is safe and responsible.

Responsible wildlife tourism is about more than just seeing animals—it's about ensuring that your interactions with wildlife are ethical, respectful, and supportive of conservation efforts. By engaging in responsible wildlife tourism, you can contribute to protecting Thailand's incredible biodiversity while enjoying meaningful and educational experiences. Whether you're visiting an elephant sanctuary, observing gibbons in their natural habitat, or participating in marine conservation, your actions can make a positive difference. Use the tips and recommendations in this chapter to ensure that your wildlife encounters are both enjoyable and responsible, and take pride in knowing that your travels are helping to protect the world's most vulnerable species.

Supporting Local Communities

As travelers, we have the power to positively impact the places we visit by supporting local communities. Sustainable tourism is about protecting the environment and fostering economic development, cultural preservation, and social empowerment for the people who call these destinations home. This section will explore the importance of supporting local communities, highlight community-based tourism projects in Thailand, discuss the benefits of engaging in community-based tourism, and provide practical tips for responsibly supporting local communities during your travels.

The Importance of Supporting Local Communities

Tourism can profoundly affect local communities, and when approached responsibly, it can be a powerful tool for positive change. Travelers can contribute to long-term economic, cultural, and social sustainability by supporting local businesses and engaging in community-based tourism.

Economic Benefits:

- **Creating Jobs and Supporting Local Businesses:** One of the most significant impacts of sustainable tourism is its ability to create jobs for local residents. Whether through homestays, local tours, or handcrafted goods, community-based tourism generates income that directly benefits the people living in the region. This economic boost helps support local businesses, fostering community growth and development.

Cultural Preservation:

- **Encouraging Traditional Crafts and Local Customs:** Tourism can also play a key role in preserving local culture and traditions. By participating in community-based tourism, travelers promote the continuation of traditional crafts, practices, and festivals. This provides economic benefits and helps ensure that these cultural practices are passed down to future generations.

Community Development:

- **Funding Education and Healthcare Projects:** Sustainable tourism initiatives often reinvest some of their profits into the local community, funding essential projects such as education, healthcare, and infrastructure development. This reinvestment helps improve the quality of life for local residents, providing long-term benefits that extend beyond the tourism industry.

Empowerment:

- **Providing Opportunities and Reducing Poverty:** By supporting community-based tourism, travelers empower local residents by providing them with opportunities for economic independence and skill development. This empowerment helps reduce poverty and gives communities more control over their futures. Through tourism, individuals gain access to training and employment that may otherwise be out of reach.

Community-Based Tourism Projects in Thailand

Thailand is home to numerous community-based tourism projects that involve and benefit local communities. These initiatives offer travelers the chance to immerse themselves in authentic cultural experiences while contributing to the well-being of the communities they visit.

CHAPTER 13: ECO-TOURISM & SUSTAINABILITY

CBT-I (Community-Based Tourism Institute):

- **Various Community Projects and Cultural Immersion:** The Community-Based Tourism Institute (CBT-I) supports a network of community-based tourism initiatives across Thailand. These projects are designed to provide authentic cultural experiences while promoting sustainable development. Visitors can participate in homestays, learn traditional crafts, and engage in Eco-tours, all while supporting local communities. CBT-I places a strong emphasis on empowering communities and preserving their cultural heritage.

Ban Talae Nok Village (Ranong):

- **Home-stays and Cultural Activities:** Located in the coastal province of Ranong, Ban Talae Nok Village offers travelers the opportunity to experience the daily life of a traditional fishing village. Visitors can stay in a local homestay, learn how to weave traditional mats, participate in fishing activities, and explore the mangrove forests. This community-based tourism initiative helps support local families and contributes to the preservation of traditional fishing practices.

Ban Talae Nok Village

Mae Kampong Village (Chiang Mai):

- **Eco-Tours and Traditional Crafts:** Nestled in the mountains near Chiang Mai, Mae Kampong Village is known for its Eco-friendly tourism practices and commitment to cultural preservation. Visitors can stay in local homestays, participate in traditional tea-making, and explore the village's lush surroundings on guided Eco-tours. The village has made a conscious effort to develop tourism to minimize its environmental impact, making it a model for sustainable community-based tourism.

Lanjia Lodge (Chiang Rai):

- **Hill Tribe Experiences and Sustainable Farming:** Lanjia Lodge, located in northern Thailand, offers travelers the chance to experience the culture of the Hmong and Lahu hill tribes. Visitors can participate in activities such as learning about traditional farming practices, enjoying cultural performances, and exploring the local environment. Lanjia Lodge is deeply committed to sustainability, supporting local communities through Eco-friendly practices and providing training and employment opportunities for residents.

Benefits of Engaging in Community-Based Tourism

Engaging in community-based tourism offers many benefits, both for travelers and the communities they visit. These experiences provide deep cultural immersion, foster sustainable practices, and contribute to meaningful, long-term change.

Authentic Experiences:

- **Deep Cultural Immersion and Personal Connections:** Community-based tourism allows travelers to experience local life authentically and meaningfully. Visitors gain a deeper understanding of the region and its people by staying with local families, participating in daily activities, and learning about cultural traditions. These personal connections create lasting memories and help foster mutual respect and understanding.

Skill-Sharing:

- **Learning and Teaching Local Crafts or Cooking:** Many community-based tourism projects offer travelers the opportunity to learn traditional skills such as weaving, pottery, or cooking. In some cases, visitors can also share their own skills, such as teaching English or offering technical assistance. This knowledge exchange helps preserve local traditions while providing residents new skills and insights.

Sustainable Practices:

- **Low-Impact Tourism and Environmental Conservation:** Community-based tourism often emphasizes sustainable practices that minimize the environmental impact of tourism. This can include Eco-friendly accommodations, sustainable farming practices, and conservation efforts. By participating in these initiatives, travelers contribute to protecting local ecosystems and supporting environmentally responsible tourism.

Long-Term Impact:

- **Supporting Ongoing Projects and Lasting Change:** One of the most rewarding aspects of community-based tourism is knowing that your visit contributes to long-term development. By supporting local businesses, participating in cultural activities, and contributing to conservation efforts, travelers help ensure that these initiatives can continue to thrive. The positive impact of your visit extends beyond your stay, contributing to lasting change in the community.

Tips for Responsibly Supporting Local Communities

When engaging with local communities, it's important to do so in a respectful, ethical way and mindful of the impact your actions may have. Here are some practical tips for supporting local communities responsibly.

Buying Local:

- **Supporting Markets and Artisans:** When purchasing souvenirs or gifts, opt for locally made products that support local artisans and businesses. Visit markets, craft cooperatives, and small shops where your money directly benefits the community. Buying handmade goods supports local economies and helps preserve traditional crafts and skills.

Participating in Volunteer Programs:

- **Ethical Volunteering and Skill-Based Contributions:** If you're interested in volunteering, choose programs prioritizing ethical practices and meaningful contributions. Look for organizations matching your skills with the community's needs, and avoid programs focusing on "voluntarism" without providing real benefits. Skill-based volunteering, such as teaching or helping with conservation projects, can have a positive and lasting impact.

Respecting Traditions:

- **Learning About and Respecting Local Customs:** Before visiting a community, take the time to learn about local customs, traditions, and social norms. Please show respect by following local etiquette, such as dressing modestly, participating in cultural rituals, and being mindful of your behavior. Respecting traditions helps foster positive relationships and ensures that your presence is welcomed and appreciated.

Providing Feedback:

- **Sharing Positive Experiences and Constructive Suggestions:** Share your feedback with the organizers after participating in community-based tourism. Positive reviews can help attract more visitors and support the initiative, while constructive suggestions can help improve the experience for future travelers. Providing feedback helps ensure that these projects continue to grow and evolve in ways that benefit both the community and visitors.

Supporting local communities through sustainable tourism is one of the most rewarding and impactful travel methods. By engaging in community-based tourism projects, travelers contribute to the preservation of cultural traditions, the empowerment of local residents, and the protection of the environment. Whether you're staying in a homestay, learning traditional crafts, or volunteering your skills, your actions can make a meaningful difference in the lives of the people you encounter. Use the tips and recommendations in this chapter to ensure that your travels in Thailand are ethical, responsible, and beneficial for the communities you visit, and take pride in knowing that your journey contributes to a more sustainable and inclusive world.

CHAPTER 14: DETAILED SAMPLE ITINERARIES

Detailed Itineraries

Thailand offers diverse experiences, from bustling city life and ancient ruins to serene beaches and lush jungles. Whether you have a week, two weeks, or a month to explore this incredible country, there's an itinerary to suit your interests and pace of travel. In this chapter, we'll provide three detailed itineraries designed to help you make the most of your time in Thailand, whether you're interested in highlights, cultural immersion, or a mix of adventure and relaxation.

One-Week Highlights Tour

This one-week itinerary is perfect for first-time visitors who want to experience the best of Thailand in a short amount of time. From the vibrant streets of Bangkok to the tranquil beaches of Phuket, this tour offers a snapshot of Thailand's most iconic destinations.

Day 1-2: Exploring Bangkok

CHAPTER 14: DETAILED SAMPLE ITINERARIES

- **Grand Palace:**
- **Detailed Visit and Historical Significance:** Start your journey with a visit to the Grand Palace, one of Bangkok's most famous landmarks. This stunning complex of buildings served as the official residence of the Kings of Siam since 1782. Take your time exploring the intricate details of the architecture and the revered Emerald Buddha at Wat Phra Kaew, and learn about the history and cultural significance of the palace.
- **Wat Pho:**
- **Reclining Buddha and Traditional Thai Massage:** Just a short walk from the Grand Palace, Wat Pho is home to the massive Reclining Buddha statue, which is 46 meters long and covered in gold leaf. After admiring the statue, treat yourself to a traditional Thai massage at the temple's massage school, known for being the birthplace of Thai massage.
- **Chatuchak Weekend Market:**
- **Extensive Shopping and Local Food Stalls:** Spend your afternoon at Chatuchak Weekend Market, one of the largest markets in the world. With over 15,000 stalls selling everything from clothing and accessories to antiques and local handicrafts, this market is a shopper's paradise. Don't miss the chance to sample street food from the various stalls scattered throughout the market.
- **Chao Phraya River Cruise:**
- **Iconic Landmarks and Evening Lights:** In the evening, unwind with a cruise along the Chao Phraya River. Gliding past Bangkok's skyline, famous landmarks like Wat Arun and the Grand Palace are illuminated against the night sky. This is a relaxing way to end your day

and take in the beauty of Bangkok from a different perspective.

Day 3: Ayutthaya Day Trip

- **Ayutthaya Historical Park:**
- **Temple Ruins and UNESCO Site:** Take a day trip to the ancient city of Ayutthaya, a UNESCO World Heritage Site. Explore the vast Ayutthaya Historical Park, where you'll find the remains of several magnificent temples and palaces that date back to the 14th century.
- **Wat Mahathat:**
- **Buddha Head Entwined in Tree Roots:** One of the most iconic sights in Ayutthaya is the Buddha head entwined in the roots of a tree at Wat Mahathat. This temple is a must-see for its unique and serene beauty, offering a glimpse into the city's past.
- **Local Market Visit:**
- **Sampling Local Delicacies:** Before returning to Bangkok, visit a local market in Ayutthaya to sample some regional delicacies. Try dishes like boat noodles, grilled river prawns, or roti sai mai (Thai-style cotton candy).
- **Return to Bangkok:**
- **Evening Relaxation and Rooftop Bar:** After a day of exploration, return to Bangkok for some relaxation. Consider ending the day with a drink at one of Bangkok's many rooftop bars, such as the Sky Bar at Lebua, where you can enjoy stunning city views.

Day 4-5: Chiang Mai Adventures

CHAPTER 14: DETAILED SAMPLE ITINERARIES

- **Doi Suthep Temple:**
- **Scenic View and Cultural Insights:** Fly to Chiang Mai and visit Doi Suthep, a mountain temple with panoramic city views. The temple is one of the most sacred in northern Thailand, and the journey up the mountain is an adventure.
- **Old City Temples:**
- **Wat Chedi Luang and Wat Phra Singh:** Spend the afternoon exploring the temples within Chiang Mai's Old City. Wat Chedi Luang is known for its massive chedi (stupa), while Wat Phra Singh is famous for its beautiful Lanna architecture and important Buddha statues.
- **Chiang Mai Night Bazaar:**
- **Shopping and Street Food:** In the evening, head to the Chiang Mai Night Bazaar, where you can shop for handicrafts, clothing, and souvenirs. The bazaar is also a great place to sample northern Thai street food, such as khao soi (coconut curry noodle soup) and sai ua (northern Thai sausage).
- **Elephant Nature Park:**
- **Ethical Elephant Interactions and Full-Day Visit:** Dedicate a whole day to visiting the Elephant Nature Park, a sanctuary for rescued elephants. Learn about the ethical treatment of elephants, observe them in their natural environment, and even participate in feeding and bathing them. This experience is both educational and deeply moving.

Day 6-7: Island Relaxation in Phuket

- **Patong Beach:**

- **Sunbathing and Water Sports:** Fly to Phuket for the final leg of your journey. Spend your first day on Patong Beach relaxing in the sun, swimming in the warm waters, or trying various water sports like jet skiing or parasailing.
- **Phi Phi Islands Day Trip:**
- **Snorkeling and Island Hopping:** Take a day trip to the Phi Phi Islands, famous for their crystal-clear waters and vibrant marine life. Go snorkeling, explore hidden coves, and enjoy a leisurely boat ride through the stunning archipelago.
- **Phuket Old Town:**
- **Heritage Buildings and Local Cuisine:** Back in Phuket, explore the historic Old Town, known for its colorful Sino-Portuguese buildings and vibrant street art. Enjoy a meal at one of the local restaurants, where you can try southern Thai specialties like massaman curry and tom som pla krabok (spicy and sour fish soup).
- **Sunset at Promthep Cape:**
- **Scenic Views and Photo Opportunities:** End your week with a visit to Promthep Cape, one of the best places in Phuket to watch the sunset. The views of the Andaman Sea are breathtaking, and it's a perfect spot to capture some memorable photos.

Two-Week Cultural Immersion

This two-week itinerary is designed for travelers who want to dive deep into the cultural and natural beauty of Thailand, with a focus on the northern and central regions.

Week 1: Northern Thailand Exploration

CHAPTER 14: DETAILED SAMPLE ITINERARIES

- **Chiang Mai:**
- **Doi Suthep, Old City Temples, Night Bazaar:** Begin your journey in Chiang Mai, where you can explore the city's rich cultural heritage. Visit Doi Suthep, wander through the Old City's temples and enjoy the vibrant Night Bazaar.
- **Chiang Rai:**
- **White Temple, Blue Temple, Night Market:** Travel to Chiang Rai, home to the striking White Temple (Wat Rong Khun) and the serene Blue Temple (Wat Rong Suea Ten). Explore the night market in the evening, where you can find unique handicrafts and local delicacies.
- **Mae Hong Son Loop:**
- **Scenic Drive and Hill Tribe Visits:** Embark on the Mae Hong Son Loop, which takes you through mountainous landscapes and charming villages. Along the way, visit hill tribe communities, where you can learn about their traditions and way of life.
- **Pai:**
- **Relaxation, Hot Springs, Pai Canyon:** Conclude your week in the laid-back town of Pai, known for its hot springs and natural beauty. Spend time relaxing in the hot springs, exploring Pai Canyon, and enjoying the town's bohemian vibe.

Week 2: Central and Eastern Thailand Discoveries

- **Sukhothai Historical Park:**
- **Ancient Ruins and Cycling Tour:** Travel to Sukhothai, where you can explore the ancient ruins of Thailand's first capital. Rent a bicycle and ride through the historical

park, discovering the well-preserved temples and statues that date back to the 13th century.

- **Lopburi:**
- **Monkey Temple and Sunflower Fields:** Continue to Lopburi, a town known for its playful monkey population. Visit the Monkey Temple (Prang Sam Yot), and if you're visiting during the right season, take a trip to the nearby sunflower fields.
- **Khao Yai National Park:**
- **Wildlife Spotting and Hiking Trails:** Explore Khao Yai National Park, a UNESCO World Heritage Site known for its diverse wildlife and lush landscapes. Go on a guided hike to spot elephants, gibbons, and hornbills, or enjoy a scenic drive through the park.
- **Chanthaburi:**
- **Gem Markets and Cathedral of the Immaculate Conception:** End your two-week journey in Chanthaburi, a town famous for its gem markets and the beautiful Cathedral of the Immaculate Conception. Spend time exploring the local markets and learning about the town's history as a trading hub.

Cultural Workshops and Classes

- **Thai Cooking Class in Chiang Mai:**
- **Traditional Recipes and Local Market Visit:** Enhance your cultural immersion by taking a Thai cooking class in Chiang Mai. Visit a local market to gather ingredients and learn how to prepare traditional dishes like pad Thai and green curry.
- **Traditional Dance Workshop:**

- **Lanna Culture and Performance:** Participate in a traditional Lanna dance workshop in Chiang Mai, where you can learn the graceful movements of northern Thai dance and understand its cultural significance.
- **Craft Workshops in Sukhothai:**
- **Pottery and Traditional Textiles:** While in Sukhothai, participate in craft workshops where you can try your hand at pottery or learn about traditional textile weaving techniques.
- **Muay Thai Class:**
- **Introduction to Thai Boxing and Basic Techniques:** Experience the excitement of Muay Thai, Thailand's national sport, by taking a beginner's class. Learn the basic techniques of Thai boxing and get a taste of this ancient martial art.

Local Festivals and Events

- **Loy Krathong:**
- **Floating Lanterns and Cultural Performances:** Plan your visit to coincide with Loy Krathong, one of Thailand's most beautiful festivals. Participate in the ritual of releasing floating lanterns onto the water and enjoy cultural performances in the evening.
- **Yi Peng:**
- **Lantern Festival in Chiang Mai and Releasing Sky Lanterns:** If you're in Chiang Mai during Yi Peng, don't miss the chance to release sky lanterns as part of this magical festival. The sight of thousands of lanterns lighting up the night sky is unforgettable.
- **Local Markets:**

- **Participating in Regional Market Days and Night Markets:** Throughout your journey, make time to visit local markets, where you can interact with vendors, sample regional foods, and purchase unique handicrafts.
- **Village Home-stays:**
- **Cultural Exchange and Daily Life Participation:** For a deeper cultural experience, consider staying in a village homestay. This will allow you to participate in daily life, from farming to cooking, and engage in meaningful cultural exchange with your hosts.

One-Month Adventure and Relaxation

For those with the luxury of time, this one-month itinerary offers a comprehensive exploration of Thailand, balancing adventure with relaxation.

Week 1-2: Comprehensive Northern and Central Thailand

- **Chiang Mai:**
- **Temples, Elephant Sanctuary, Trekking:** Start your month-long journey in Chiang Mai, where you can explore temples, visit an ethical elephant sanctuary, and embark on trekking adventures in the surrounding hills.
- **Chiang Rai:**
- **Temples and Golden Triangle:** Travel to Chiang Rai to see the famous White and Blue Temples and visit the Golden Triangle, where the borders of Thailand, Laos, and Myanmar meet.
- **Sukhothai:**
- **Historical Park and Cycling:** Continue to Sukhothai

for a deep dive into Thailand's ancient history. Spend your days cycling through the historical park, marveling at the well-preserved ruins.
- **Ayutthaya:**
- **Historical Park and River Cruise:** Visit Ayutthaya to explore its UNESCO-listed historical park and take a river cruise around the ancient city, soaking in the rich history and culture.

Week 3: Eastern Thailand and the Gulf Islands

- **Koh Chang:**
- **Beaches, Snorkeling, Mu Ko Chang National Park:** Head to Eastern Thailand and start your island-hopping adventure in Koh Chang. Enjoy the pristine beaches, go snorkeling, and explore the natural beauty of Mu Ko Chang National Park.
- **Koh Mak:**
- **Quiet Island Life and Cycling:** Continue to the tranquil island of Koh Mak, where you can experience quiet island life. Rent a bicycle and explore the island's coconut plantations, sandy beaches, and small fishing villages.
- **Koh Kood:**
- **Waterfalls and Diving:** Visit Koh Kood, known for its stunning waterfalls and excellent diving opportunities. Spend your days exploring the underwater world or relaxing by the island's natural pools.
- **Pattaya:**
- **Sanctuary of Truth and Coral Island Day Trip:** End your week in Pattaya, where you can visit the ornate Sanctuary of Truth, a unique wooden structure dedicated

to traditional art and philosophy. Take a day trip to Coral Island for some sunbathing and water sports.

Week 4: Southern Thailand Adventure and Relaxation

- **Krabi:**
- **Rock Climbing at Railay and Island Hopping:** In Krabi, challenge yourself with rock climbing at Railay Beach, known for its dramatic limestone cliffs. Spend your afternoon island hopping and visiting Chicken Island and Poda Island.
- **Phuket:**
- **Beaches and Old Town Exploration:** Relax on the beautiful beaches of Phuket or explore the island's Old Town, known for its Sino-Portuguese architecture and vibrant street art.
- **Koh Phi Phi:**
- **Snorkeling, Maya Bay, Viking Cave:** Discover the natural beauty of Koh Phi Phi, where you can snorkel in crystal-clear waters, visit the famous Maya Bay, and explore the ancient Viking Cave.
- **Similan Islands:**
- **Diving and Marine Life Exploration:** Conclude your journey with a visit to the Similan Islands, one of Thailand's top diving destinations. Dive into the clear waters to explore vibrant coral reefs and diverse marine life.

Balance of Adventure and Relaxation

- **Trekking:**
- **Chiang Mai and Khao Sok National Park:** Include

CHAPTER 14: DETAILED SAMPLE ITINERARIES

trekking in your itinerary to taste Thailand's natural beauty. In addition to Chiang Mai, consider a trek in Khao Sok National Park, home to one of the world's oldest rainforests.

- **Water Activities:**
- **Snorkeling, Diving, Kayaking:** Incorporate plenty of water activities into your itinerary, from snorkeling and diving in the Andaman Sea to kayaking through mangroves and along coastlines.
- **Beach Days:**
- **Koh Samui, Koh Tao, Phuket:** Balance your adventures with days spent lounging on the beaches of Koh Samui, Koh Tao, and Phuket. Each of these islands offers its own unique charm and opportunities for relaxation.
- **Spa Treatments:**
- **Traditional Thai Massages and Wellness Retreats:** Throughout your journey, take time to indulge in traditional Thai massages and wellness treatments. Thailand is known for its spa culture, and visiting a wellness retreat can be a rejuvenating experience.

Whether you have a week, two weeks, or a month to explore Thailand, each itinerary offers a carefully curated journey through the country's most beautiful and culturally rich destinations. From the bustling streets of Bangkok to the serene beaches of Phuket, from the ancient ruins of Sukhothai to the lush jungles of Chiang Mai, there's something for every traveler in Thailand. Use these itineraries as a guide to plan your own adventure, ensuring that you experience the best of what this incredible country has to offer.

CHAPTER 15: PRACTICAL AND UP-TO-DATE TRAVEL ADVICE

Practical and Up-to-Date Travel Advice

When planning a trip to Thailand, having practical and up-to-date travel advice can make all the difference in ensuring a smooth and enjoyable journey. From knowing what to pack to navigating the healthcare system, being well-prepared allows you to focus on Thailand's beauty and adventure. In this chapter, we'll cover essential packing lists tailored to different types of travelers, advice on navigating Thai healthcare and handling emergencies, and tips for staying healthy while on the road. We will also cover apps to use when traveling and tips on how to stay connected while away.

Essential Packing Lists for Thailand

Packing for Thailand can vary depending on the season, the type of trip you're taking, and your personal needs. Here's a comprehensive guide to help you pack efficiently and ensure you have everything you need for a comfortable and enjoyable stay.

CHAPTER 15: PRACTICAL AND UP-TO-DATE TRAVEL ADVICE

General Packing Checklist

This checklist covers the basics that all travelers should consider when packing for Thailand:

Lightweight Clothing:

- **Breathable Fabrics, Comfortable Wear:** Thailand's tropical climate means you'll want to pack lightweight, breathable clothing. Opt for cotton, linen, or moisture-wicking fabrics that keep you cool in the heat. Consider packing a mix of casual and modest clothing, especially if you plan to visit temples or rural areas where conservative dress is expected.

Travel Documents:

- **Passport, Visa, Travel Insurance:** Ensure your passport is valid for at least six months beyond your planned departure date. You may need a visa to enter Thailand depending on your nationality, so check the requirements before you travel. It's also essential to have comprehensive travel insurance that covers medical emergencies, trip cancellations, and any activities you plan to participate in.

Personal Care Items:

- **Toiletries, Sunscreen, Mosquito Repellent:** Bring travel-sized toiletries, including shampoo, conditioner, toothpaste, and soap. Sunscreen is a must, as Thailand's sun can be intense, and mosquito repellent is crucial to avoid bites, especially in the evening or in more rural areas.

Electronics:

- **Adapter, Power Bank, and Chargers:** Thailand uses Type C and Type A electrical outlets, so bring a universal adapter if your devices use different plugs. A power bank is handy for keeping your phone charged on the go, and don't forget chargers for your phone, camera, and other electronics.

Specialized Packing Lists for Different Traveler Types

Tailoring your packing list to your travel style and needs can help you prepare more effectively:

Solo Travelers:

- **Safety Items, Lightweight Luggage:** Solo travelers should consider packing a few extra safety items, such as a personal alarm, a doorstop for added security in your accommodation, and a copy of essential documents. Keep your luggage light and easy to manage, especially if you plan to move around frequently.

CHAPTER 15: PRACTICAL AND UP-TO-DATE TRAVEL ADVICE

Families:

- **Kid-Friendly Snacks, Entertainment, Diapers:** Traveling with children requires more preparation. Pack plenty of snacks to keep the little ones satisfied between meals and entertainment, such as coloring books, tablets with games or movies, and favorite toys. If you're traveling with a baby or toddler, don't forget diapers, wipes, and a portable changing mat.

Adventure Seekers:

- **Trekking Gear, Water Shoes, and Dry Bags:** For those planning outdoor adventures, such as trekking, diving, or kayaking, specialized gear is necessary. Bring sturdy hiking boots, water shoes for rocky beaches or river crossings, and a dry bag to keep your belongings safe and dry during water activities.

Seasonal Packing Considerations

Thailand's climate varies by season, so adjust your packing list based on when you'll be visiting:

Cool Season (November to February):

- **Light Jackets, Layers for Varying Temperatures:** While the cold season is still warm by most standards, temperatures can drop in the evenings, especially in the northern regions. You can pack a light jacket or sweater and consider layers that can be easily added or removed.

Hot Season (March to May):

- **Sun Protection, Hydration Solutions:** The hot season in Thailand can be intense, with high temperatures and humidity. Bring extra sun protection, including sunscreen, hats, and sunglasses. Staying hydrated is key, so consider carrying a reusable water bottle with a built-in filter.

Rainy Season (June to October):

- **Waterproof Gear and Quick-Dry Clothing:** Sudden downpours are expected during the rainy season. Pack a lightweight rain jacket or poncho, waterproof footwear, and quick-dry clothing to stay comfortable in wet conditions. An umbrella is also a good idea for quick cover.

Practical Tips for Efficient Packing

Efficient packing can save space in your luggage and make your travels more convenient:

Packing Cubes:

- **Organization and Space-Saving:** Packing cubes are a great way to organize your clothing and accessories while maximizing space. Use different cubes for different categories, such as tops, bottoms, and undergarments, to keep everything neat and easy to find.

CHAPTER 15: PRACTICAL AND UP-TO-DATE TRAVEL ADVICE

Rolling Clothes:

- **Reducing Wrinkles, Maximizing Space:** Rolling your clothes instead of folding them can help reduce wrinkles and save space in your suitcase. This method is particularly useful for lightweight fabrics like t-shirts and shorts.

Versatile Clothing:

- **Mix-and-Match Outfits:** Choose clothing items that can be easily mixed and matched to create multiple outfits. Neutral colors and simple designs work best for this purpose, allowing you to dress up or down as needed.

Minimalist Packing:

- **Essentials Only, Avoiding Excess:** Try to limit your packing to the essentials to avoid over-packing. Consider what you can realistically wear during your trip and avoid bringing items "just in case." Focus on multi-purpose items, such as a sarong that can double as a beach cover-up or a light blanket.

Navigating Thai Healthcare and Emergencies

You must understand how to navigate the healthcare system and handle emergencies in Thailand, which is crucial for any traveler. Here's what you need to know to stay safe and healthy during your trip.

Overview of the Thai Healthcare System

Thailand has a well-developed healthcare system with various facilities offering quality care. Here's a brief overview:

Types of Facilities:

- **Public Hospitals, Private Hospitals, Clinics:** Thailand offers a mix of public and private healthcare facilities. Public hospitals provide affordable care but may be crowded and have longer wait times. Private hospitals, on the other hand, offer higher standards of care, shorter wait times, and more amenities, often catering to international patients. Clinics, especially in tourist areas, are also widely available, offering basic healthcare services.

Quality of Care:

- **Standards and Language Barriers:** The quality of care in Thailand's private hospitals is generally excellent, with many facilities meeting international standards. However, language barriers can be an issue, especially in public hospitals. Most private hospitals in tourist areas have English-speaking staff, but having a translation app on hand is always a good idea.

Costs:

- **Payment Methods and Insurance Coverage:** Healthcare costs in Thailand are relatively low compared to Western countries, but it's important to have travel insurance that covers medical expenses. Most private hospitals require payment upfront or proof of insurance. Be sure to carry a credit card or enough cash to cover any immediate expenses.

Finding and Choosing Healthcare Facilities

If you need medical attention during your trip, here's how to find and choose the right facility:

Reputable Hospitals:

- **Bumrungrad International Hospital, Bangkok Hospital:** For high-quality care, consider visiting reputable private hospitals such as Bumrungrad International Hospital in Bangkok, known for its world-class facilities and services, or Bangkok Hospital, which has branches in major cities across Thailand.

Clinics:

- **Local Clinics, International Clinics in Tourist Areas:** Local clinics are convenient for minor ailments or routine check-ups. In tourist areas, you'll also find international clinics that cater specifically to travelers, offering English-speaking staff and a higher standard of care.

Pharmacies:

- **Availability and Over-the-Counter Medications:** Pharmacies are widely available in Thailand, with many open 24 hours in major cities. You can find a range of over-the-counter medications, including pain relievers, antihistamines, and antibiotics. Pharmacists are usually knowledgeable and can provide advice on minor health issues.

Handling Medical Emergencies

In the event of a medical emergency, follow these steps:

Emergency Numbers:

- **1669 for Medical Emergencies, 1155 for Tourist Police:** The emergency number for medical assistance in Thailand is 1669, where you can request an ambulance or other urgent care. For non-medical emergencies, such as theft or accidents, you can contact the Tourist Police at 1155, who are trained to assist foreign visitors.

First Response:

- **Basic First Aid and Stabilizing the Situation:** If you're involved in or witness an emergency, provide basic first aid if you're able. This might include stopping bleeding, performing CPR, or stabilizing an injury until professional help arrives.

CHAPTER 15: PRACTICAL AND UP-TO-DATE TRAVEL ADVICE

Contacting Insurance:

- **Claim Procedures and Hospital Admissions:** As soon as possible, you can contact your travel insurance provider to report the incident and get guidance on the next steps. If necessary, they can assist with hospital admissions, payment guarantees, and emergency evacuation.

Language Assistance:

- **Using Translation Apps and Seeking Help from Locals:** If language barriers are a concern, use a translation app to communicate with medical staff. In tourist areas, you can also seek help from hotel staff or local guides who may speak English and can assist you in navigating the situation.

Preventive Health Measures

To stay healthy and avoid common health issues while traveling in Thailand, consider the following preventive measures:

Vaccinations:

- **Hepatitis A, Typhoid, Optional Ones Like Rabies:** Before traveling to Thailand, check with your healthcare provider about recommended vaccinations. Hepatitis A and typhoid are commonly recommended for travelers, while rabies and Japanese encephalitis may be advised for those planning extended stays or rural visits.

Food and Water Safety:

- **Eating at Reputable Places, Avoiding Tap Water:** To avoid food-borne illnesses, eat at reputable restaurants and food stalls where you can see food being prepared fresh. Avoid tap water and instead drink bottled or filtered water. Be cautious with ice and raw foods, such as salads and unpeeled fruits.

Sun Protection:

- **Sunscreen, Hats, Hydration:** The sun in Thailand can be intense, so protect yourself by wearing sunscreen with high SPF, a wide-brimmed hat, and sunglasses. Drink plenty of water throughout the day to stay hydrated, especially if you're spending time outdoors.

Mosquito Precautions:

- **Repellent, Mosquito Nets, Covering Up:** Mosquitoes can be a nuisance; in some areas, they can carry diseases like dengue fever or malaria. Use insect repellent, especially in the evening, sleep under a mosquito net if your accommodation doesn't have one, and wear long sleeves and pants in mosquito-prone areas.

Being well-prepared with practical travel advice can make your trip to Thailand smooth, safe, and enjoyable. By packing smartly, understanding the local healthcare system, and taking preventive health measures, you'll be ready to fully embrace the adventure that awaits you. Keep this chapter handy as you

CHAPTER 15: PRACTICAL AND UP-TO-DATE TRAVEL ADVICE

plan your journey, and you'll have the confidence to explore Thailand with peace of mind, knowing that you're prepared for whatever comes your way.

Using Travel Apps and Online Resources

In today's digital age, travel apps and online resources have become essential tools for navigating new destinations, planning trips, and staying connected. Whether you're looking for transportation options, accommodation, or local dining recommendations, the right apps and websites can enhance your travel experience in Thailand. In this section, we'll explore some of the most useful travel apps, online resources, social media platforms, and tips for staying connected during your journey.

Essential Travel Apps for Navigating Thailand

When traveling in Thailand, having the right apps on your smartphone can make everything from finding your way around to booking accommodation much easier. Here are some must-have apps to help you navigate Thailand efficiently and enjoyably.

Transportation:

- **Grab for Ride-Sharing:** Grab is Southeast Asia's leading ride-sharing app, similar to Uber, and is widely used in Thailand. Grab provides reliable and affordable transportation options, whether you need a car, taxi, or even a motorbike. The app allows you to book rides in

advance, track your driver, and pay securely through the app, eliminating the need to carry cash.
- **Google Maps for Navigation:** Google Maps is an essential app for navigating Thailand's cities and countryside. It offers accurate, real-time directions whether you're walking, driving, or using public transportation. You can also use the app to explore nearby attractions, find restaurants, and check reviews.

Accommodation:

- **Airbnb for Unique Stays:** If you're looking for more unique or homey accommodations, Airbnb offers many options, from cozy apartments to luxurious villas. The app allows you to communicate directly with hosts, read reviews from previous guests, and find places that match your specific needs and budget.
- **Booking.com for Hotels:** Booking.com is a trusted platform for finding hotels in Thailand, offering a vast selection of properties ranging from budget guesthouses to five-star resorts. The app is user-friendly and often features exclusive mobile deals. It also provides free cancellation options on many bookings, which is helpful if your plans change.

Dining:

- **Eatigo for Restaurant Discounts:** Eatigo is a dining app that offers discounts of up to 50% at restaurants across Thailand. The app lets you browse restaurants by location, cuisine, or discount level and book your table directly through the app. This is a great way to enjoy some of Thailand's best dining experiences at a fraction of the cost.

- **HappyCow for Vegetarian Options:** If you're vegetarian or vegan, HappyCow is an invaluable resource for finding plant-based dining options. The app lists vegetarian and vegan restaurants and places that offer good vegetarian options, complete with reviews and directions.

Translation:

- **Google Translate for Language Assistance:** Language barriers can be challenging when traveling in Thailand, but Google Translate can help bridge the gap. The app offers text translation, voice translation, and even a camera function that can translate text into images, such as signs or menus. It's particularly useful in rural areas where English is less commonly spoken.

Online Resources for Trip Planning

Planning a trip to Thailand involves gathering information from a variety of sources. The following websites and online platforms provide valuable insights, tips, and tools to help you plan a seamless and enjoyable trip.

Travel Forums:

- **Trip Advisor:** Trip Advisor is a well-established platform where travelers share reviews and advice on hotels, attractions, and restaurants. The forums are particularly helpful for getting personalized advice from other travelers who have been to Thailand recently.
- **Lonely Planet's Thorn Tree:** Thorn Tree is a popular travel forum run by Lonely Planet, where travelers exchange tips and experiences. It's a great place to ask questions, find itinerary suggestions, and connect with other travelers heading to Thailand.

Government Websites:

- **Thai Tourism Board:** The official Thai Tourism Board website offers a wealth of information on Thailand's attractions, events, and travel tips. It's an excellent starting point for anyone planning a trip to the country, providing up-to-date information on visa requirements, travel advisories, and cultural insights.
- **Visa Information Sites:** Websites like the Thai Embassy or consulate in your home country provide detailed information on visa requirements, application processes, and entry regulations. This is essential reading to ensure you have the correct visa for your stay in Thailand.

CHAPTER 15: PRACTICAL AND UP-TO-DATE TRAVEL ADVICE

Travel Blogs:

- **Detailed Itineraries and Personal Experiences:** Travel blogs are a rich source of inspiration and practical advice, often offering detailed itineraries, tips on off-the-beaten-path locations, and personal anecdotes. Blogs like The Blonde Abroad, Nomadic Matt, and Travelfish are popular choices for Thailand-specific content.

Booking Platforms:

- **Skyscanner for Flights:** Skyscanner is a powerful flight comparison tool that helps you find the best deals on flights to and from Thailand. You can search by date and airline or even find the cheapest month to fly.
- **12Go Asia for Transport Tickets:** 12Go Asia is an excellent resource for booking transportation in Thailand, including trains, buses, ferries, and flights. The platform allows you to compare schedules and prices and book tickets online, making planning your travel between destinations easy.

Social Media and Travel Communities

Social media platforms and online communities are great resources for real-time travel tips, local insights, and connecting with other travelers. Here's how to leverage these platforms during your trip to Thailand.

Facebook Groups:

- **Thailand Travel Groups and Expat Communities:** Facebook groups are a valuable resource for connecting with other travelers and expats in Thailand. Groups like "Thailand Travelers" and "Expats in Thailand" are active communities where you can ask questions, share experiences, and get advice from people who are currently in the country.

Instagram:

- **Following Travel Influencers and Location Tags:** Instagram is a fantastic tool for discovering Thailand's beautiful places and hidden gems. Follow travel influencers who focus on Thailand, and explore location tags to find popular spots and get ideas for your itinerary. You can also use Instagram's save feature to bookmark posts for future reference.

Reddit:

- **r/Thailand and r/solotravel for Advice and Discussions:** Reddit is home to several travel-related communities, including r/Thailand, where users share tips, experiences, and news about Thailand. r/solotravel is another useful subreddit for solo travelers seeking advice and support from a like-minded community.

CHAPTER 15: PRACTICAL AND UP-TO-DATE TRAVEL ADVICE

YouTube:

- **Vlogs, Destination Guides, Travel Tips:** YouTube is an excellent platform for visual learners who prefer video content. You can search for vlogs and destination guides about Thailand to get a sense of what to expect and to pick up practical tips. Channels like Lost LeBlanc, Migrationology, and The Endless Adventure are popular choices for Thailand travel content.

Tips for Staying Connected

Staying connected while traveling in Thailand is crucial for accessing online resources, keeping in touch with loved ones, and navigating your trip. Here are some tips to help you stay connected seamlessly.

SIM Cards:

- **Local SIM Options and Data Packages:** One of the most convenient ways to stay connected in Thailand is to purchase a local SIM card upon arrival. Companies like AIS, DTAC, and TrueMove offer affordable data packages with reliable 4G coverage nationwide. SIM cards can be purchased at the airport or from convenience stores like 7-Eleven.

Wi-Fi Hotspots:

- **Portable Devices and Free Wi-Fi Locations:** If you prefer not to switch SIM cards, consider renting a portable Wi-Fi hotspot device. These devices allow you to connect multiple devices to the internet and are available for rent at the airport or online. Additionally, many cafes, hotels, and shopping centers in Thailand offer free Wi-Fi, which can be handy for checking maps or making reservations.

Offline Resources:

- **Downloadable Maps and Travel Guides:** To ensure you can never access important information, download offline maps and travel guides before you leave. Apps like Google Maps and Maps.me allow you to download maps for offline use, and you can also download PDFs of travel guides and essential documents.

Communication Apps:

- **Whats App, LINE for Staying in Touch:** Communication apps like Whats App and LINE are widely used in Thailand to stay in touch with friends, family, and local contacts. These apps allow free voice and video calls over Wi-Fi or mobile data and are helpful for messaging and sharing your location.

Incorporating the right travel apps and online resources into your travel planning can significantly enhance your experience in Thailand. Whether you're navigating the streets

CHAPTER 15: PRACTICAL AND UP-TO-DATE TRAVEL ADVICE

of Bangkok, booking accommodation, or finding the best local eats, these tools provide convenience, save time, and help you make the most of your trip. By staying connected and leveraging the wealth of information available online, you'll be well-equipped to explore Thailand with confidence and ease. Keep this chapter as a reference to ensure you have the best digital resources at your fingertips throughout your journey.

CHAPTER 16: INSIDER TIPS FROM THAI LOCALS

Insider Tips from Thai Locals

One of the most enriching aspects of traveling in Thailand is connecting with locals and learning from their deep knowledge and insights. While guidebooks and travel apps are helpful, there's nothing quite like the advice you get from people who know the country intimately. In this chapter, we'll explore the value of local knowledge, share insider tips from Thai locals, and discuss how you can engage with locals to enhance your experience. You'll also hear stories of how connecting with locals has led to unforgettable moments during my friend's travels in Thailand.

The Value of Local Knowledge

Local knowledge can unlock experiences beyond typical tourist attractions, offering a more authentic and enriching journey. Thai locals are often generous with their time and advice, providing insights that can deepen your understanding of the country and its culture.

CHAPTER 16: INSIDER TIPS FROM THAI LOCALS

Hidden Gems:

- **Lesser-Known Attractions, Local Favorites:** While Thailand has many famous landmarks, countless hidden gems often fly under the radar of most tourists. These might include secluded beaches, quiet temples, or off-the-beaten-path markets that only locals frequent. Thai locals can point you toward these treasures, offering you a more personal and unique experience of the country.

Cultural Nuances:

- **Understanding Deeper Cultural Practices:** Thailand's culture is rich and complex, with many subtle customs and traditions that aren't always obvious to outsiders. Local insights can help you understand these more profound cultural practices, such as the significance of the "wai" greeting, the importance of respecting monks, and the etiquette required when visiting temples.

Food Recommendations:

- **Best Local Dishes and Where to Try Them:** Thailand is a food lover's paradise, but knowing where to find the best local dishes can be tricky. Locals can steer you away from tourist traps and toward the most authentic street food stalls, local restaurants, and hidden eateries where you can try dishes like khao soi in Chiang Mai, boat noodles in Ayutthaya, or som tum (papaya salad) in Isaan.

Specific Tips from Thai Locals

Here are some actionable insider tips from Thai locals that can help you make the most of your trip:

Best Time to Visit Popular Sites:

- **Avoiding Crowds and Optimal Times:** Many of Thailand's most popular attractions, such as the Grand Palace or Wat Pho, can get incredibly crowded during the day. Locals suggest visiting these sites either early in the morning or late in the afternoon to avoid the largest crowds. For example, arriving at Wat Pho right when it opens will allow you to experience the Reclining Buddha in peaceful solitude before the tour buses arrive.

Local Etiquette:

- **Do's and Don'ts and Respectful Behavior:** Thai culture places a strong emphasis on respect, especially toward elders, religious figures, and the monarchy. Locals advise that when visiting temples, you should always dress modestly—covering your shoulders and knees—and remove your shoes before entering temple buildings. When greeting people, the traditional wai (placing your hands together and bowing your head slightly) is polite, especially when meeting elders or in formal situations.

CHAPTER 16: INSIDER TIPS FROM THAI LOCALS

Shopping Tips:

- **Where to Find Quality Goods and How to Haggle:** Thai markets are a shopper's dream, but haggling is an art. Locals suggest being polite but firm when negotiating prices. Start by offering about 60-70% of the asking price and work up. Smiling during negotiations is also good—Thai culture values a positive and friendly demeanor. For quality goods, locals often recommend checking out weekend markets or artisanal shops rather than tourist-heavy areas, as the quality tends to be better and prices are more reasonable.

Safety Advice:

- **Areas to Avoid and Common Scams:** While Thailand is generally a safe country for travelers, locals recommend being cautious in certain areas, especially at night. Stick to well-lit streets, avoid secluded areas, and be mindful of your belongings in crowded places. When it comes to common scams, be wary of tuk-tuk drivers offering "city tours" at unusually low prices—these often include unwanted stops at gem shops or tailors where you'll feel pressured to buy. Always agree on a price before getting into a tuk-tuk or taxi, or use ride-hailing apps like Grab for transparency.

Connecting with Locals: How to Engage for Deeper Insights

Engaging with Thai locals can greatly enhance your travel experience by offering you an insider's perspective on the culture, food, and customs. Here's how to connect with locals during your trip:

Language Learning:

- **Basic Thai Phrases and Language Exchange Apps:** Learning a few basic Thai phrases can go a long way in building rapport with locals. Simple greetings like "Sawasdee" (hello) and "Khob Khun" (thank you) are always appreciated. Language exchange apps like HelloTalk or Tandem can also help you connect with locals who are eager to practice their English while teaching you Thai.

Participating in Local Activities:

- **Festivals and Community Events:** Thailand is home to numerous vibrant festivals throughout the year, such as Songkran (the Thai New Year water festival) and Loy Krathong (the festival of lights). Participating in these festivals alongside locals is a great way to immerse yourself in the culture. Community events, like local markets or temple fairs, also provide opportunities to meet and engage with Thai people in a more relaxed setting.

CHAPTER 16: INSIDER TIPS FROM THAI LOCALS

Staying in Local Accommodations:

- **Home Stays and Guesthouses:** Choosing to stay in a local homestay or guesthouse rather than a hotel can lead to more meaningful interactions with locals. Hosts often go out of their way to make you feel welcome, and staying with a family can give you insight into daily Thai life. Many homestays also include homemade meals, providing you with an authentic taste of local cuisine.

Guided Tours:

- **Hiring Local Guides and Community-Based Tourism:** Hiring a local guide can enhance your experience by providing you with expert knowledge of the area. Community-based tourism initiatives, where local communities offer guided tours, workshops, and cultural activities, allow you to directly support local economies while gaining a deeper understanding of Thailand's culture and traditions.

Stories of Meaningful Local Interactions

Here are a few stories I've heard from friends who have traveled to Thailand that highlight how connecting with locals enhanced their experience:

Dinner Invitations:

- **Being Invited to a Local's Home:** A few friends befriended a local vendor at the night market in Chiang Mai. After several conversations over a few days, he invited them to his home for dinner with his family. It was one of the most memorable experiences of their trip—sharing a home-cooked meal, learning about his life in Chiang Mai, and getting a glimpse into the warmth and hospitality that defines Thai culture.

Festival Participation:

- **Joining in Songkran Celebrations:** While in Thailand during the Songkran festival, my friends were swept up in the water-throwing festivities. Locals eagerly included them in the celebrations, handing them buckets of water to join in the playful water fights. It was a joyful and immersive experience that connected them to the spirit of Thai culture and made them feel like a part of the community.

Learning Traditions:

- **Hands-On Experience with Thai Crafts:** My friends participated in a traditional umbrella-making workshop in a small village near Chiang Rai. A local artisan patiently guided them through each step, from carving the bamboo to painting intricate designs on the umbrella's fabric. By the end of the day, they had created a beautiful keepsake and gained a deeper appreciation for the skill and artistry involved in this traditional craft.

Shared Meals:

- **Trying Local Dishes with New Friends:** On one occasion, my friends joined a group of locals for a casual meal at a street food stall in Bangkok. They introduced them to dishes they had never tried, such as pla pao (grilled fish) and gaeng som (sour curry). The meal was filled with laughter, conversation, and generous food sharing. It reminded them that some of the best travel memories are made around the dinner table, surrounded by new friends.

There's no better way to experience Thailand than through the eyes of its people. Local knowledge can unlock hidden gems, provide deeper cultural understanding, and lead to unforgettable experiences. Whether it's through a simple conversation, participating in a festival, or staying in a local homestay, engaging with Thai locals will enrich your journey in ways that no guidebook can. Embrace the opportunities to connect with locals during your travels—you'll walk away with valuable insights, lifelong memories, and friendships.

CONCLUSION

As we reach the end of this guide, I hope the journey through these pages has left you feeling empowered and inspired to explore Thailand's beautiful and diverse country. The purpose of this book has always been clear: to provide first-time travelers with a comprehensive, accessible, and enjoyable guide that simplifies the planning process and enhances their travel experience. Whether you dream of bustling cities, serene beaches, or rich cultural experiences, this guide was designed to help you navigate your adventure quickly and confidently.

From the beginning, this book has aimed to demystify the experience of traveling in Thailand. By offering practical advice, insider tips, and budget-friendly hacks, I've sought to equip you with the knowledge and tools needed to make the most of your journey. Thailand is a country that can seem overwhelming at first, but with the proper preparation and insights, you'll find it to be an incredibly welcoming and rewarding destination.

The vision behind this guide is to make your travel experience as smooth and enriching as possible. As a first-time traveler, I wanted to ensure that you feel confident in exploring Thailand, discovering its hidden gems, and immersing yourself in

CONCLUSION

its rich culture. This book was crafted to provide a road map to the country's must-see attractions while highlighting the lesser-known destinations that make Thailand unique.

Throughout the chapters, we've covered everything from planning your trip and navigating transportation to exploring cultural landmarks and engaging with locals. We delved into the rich history of Thailand, explored its vibrant festivals, and uncovered its stunning natural beauty. Here are some of the key takeaways:

- **Stress-Free Planning:** With detailed itineraries and practical tips, you can plan a trip that suits your interests and pace. From packing lists to visa requirements, every aspect of preparation has been covered to ensure a smooth journey.
- **Discovering Hidden Gems:** Beyond the popular tourist spots, this guide has introduced you to lesser-known attractions, from secluded beaches in the south to quiet temples in the north. These hidden gems offer a more authentic and intimate experience of Thailand.
- **Maximizing Your Budget:** Travel doesn't have to break the bank. With advice on budget accommodations, affordable dining options, and money-saving tips for sightseeing, you can make the most of your budget without sacrificing the quality of your experience.

As you embark on your adventure, it's important to remember the impact of your travels on the environment and local communities. Thailand has deep-rooted traditions and a strong sense of respect, especially towards its culture, religion, and monarchy. By being mindful of cultural etiquette, supporting local businesses, and practicing sustainable travel, you'll help preserve the beauty and heritage of Thailand for future generations. Simple acts, like using Eco-friendly accommodations, avoiding single-use plastics, and participating in community-based tourism, can make a significant difference.

Now that you've read this guide, it's time to take the first step in planning your trip to Thailand. Use the insights and tips in these pages to craft an itinerary that speaks to your interests, whether an action-packed adventure, cultural exploration, or relaxing retreat. The possibilities are endless, and the experience will undoubtedly be one of the most memorable of your life.

As you prepare for your adventure, remember that travel is as much about the journey as the destination. Embrace the unexpected, connect with locals, and immerse yourself in the rich tapestry of Thai culture. With the knowledge and tools from this guide, you're well-prepared to explore Thailand with confidence and excitement. Let your curiosity guide you, and let the wonders of Thailand unfold before you.

Your adventure awaits—go forth and discover the magic of Thailand!

REVIEW

Enjoyed the Trip? Review the Guide!

Hi there, fellow traveler!

We hope *Explore Thailand* by Wanderlust Wren has helped you plan your exciting adventure or inspired you to discover the wonders of this beautiful country. Whether you've already been to Thailand or are just dreaming about it, we'd love to hear from you!

Leaving a review is like sharing your travel story—it helps future readers and travelers know what to expect and lets us know how we did. Plus, your review can help more people find and enjoy this guide!

What Can You Share in Your Review?

- What did you like most about *Explore Thailand*?
- Did the tips and advice help you plan your trip?
- What hidden gems or fun facts were your favorite?
- Any fun or helpful stories from your travels?

How to Leave a Review: It's easy! Head to where you bought the book (like Amazon or Goodreads, or by scanning the QR Code at the bottom), find *Explore Thailand*, and let everyone know what you think. Whether a few words or a complete story, your review makes a big difference.

Thank you for sharing this journey with us. Your feedback is crucial, and we can't wait to hear about your adventures!

Safe travels, and until our next adventure,
  Wanderlust Wren ✈

REVIEW

HELP SUPPORT THE AUTHOR BY
LEAVING AN HONEST REVIEW!

WWW.WANDERLUST-WREN.COM

REFERENCES

References:

Baker, M. J., & Cameron, E. (2008). *Exploring destinations: Thailand*. Oxford University Press.

Cohen, E. (2019). *The impact of tourism on Thailand: Growth, challenges, and future prospects*. Routledge.

Cummings, J., & Elliott, J. (2017). *Thailand: The essential guide to customs and culture* (3rd ed.). Kuperard.

Lonely Planet. (2023). *Thailand travel guide* (16th ed.). Lonely Planet.

Smith, T. (2016). *Cultural insights for travelers: Understanding Thai traditions*. Tuttle Publishing.

Thai Tourism Authority. (2024). *Amazing Thailand: Official travel guide*. Retrieved from https://www.tourismthailand.org/

Tourism Authority of Thailand. (2024). *Thailand festivals and events calendar*. Retrieved from https://www.tourismthailand.org/What-News-Events

Trip Advisor. (2024). *Thailand travel forum*. Retrieved from https://www.tripadvisor.com/ShowForum-g293915-i3686-Thailand.html

U.S. Department of State. (2024). *Thailand country information*. Retrieved from https://travel.state.gov/content/travel/en/international-travel/International-Travel-Country-Information-Pages/Thailand.html

Warren, P., & Stevens, H. (2022). *Thailand's hidden gems: Off-the-beaten-path adventures*. Rough Guides.

About the Author

Wanderlust Wren, a dynamic 37-year-old flight attendant and travel enthusiast, is fueled by a profound passion for exploring the world and sharing her experiences through captivating travel books. She is also a new mom with a blended family and has found that writing books to help parents navigate the changes in their lives has been meaningful and a newfound passion.

Ms. Wren's books are more than just itineraries; they are windows into the heart of each destination or experience through the eyes of a flight attendant and mother. Her writing transcends the mundane, offering readers a vicarious adventure and encouraging them to step out of their comfort zones.

Join Wanderlust Wren on a journey where every page beckons you to uncover, experience, and embrace the diversity of our world and the complexities of family dynamics!

You can connect with me on:
- https://www.wanderlust-wren.com
- https://www.facebook.com/wanderlustwren

Also by Wanderlust Wren

Wanderlust Wren is a passionate storyteller and seasoned traveler with a heart full of adventures. With a pen and a map in the other, Wren crafts captivating travel guides that inspire wanderers of all ages. Beyond the world of exploration, Wren delves into the complexities of family life, offering insightful and heartwarming books that resonate with readers. As a creative soul, Wren also brings joy to young minds through enchanting children's books. Whether guiding readers through the bustling streets of Bangkok or navigating the dynamics of a blended family, Wanderlust Wren's stories are filled with warmth, wisdom, and a touch of magic.

The Ultimate Travel Guide to the Amalfi Coast of Italy

Whispers of Amalfi: Let Your Wanderlust Guide You to Paradise! Have you ever dreamt of strolling through cliff side villages with the scent of lemon groves in the air? Are you tired of ordinary vacations? Are you ready to discover the hidden gems of the Amalfi Coast? Are you craving a travel experience that blends history, culture, and breathtaking scenery? Have you ever wondered how to turn your Amalfi dreams into a reality without breaking the bank? Are you curious about the untold stories that await you along the winding roads of the Amalfi Coast? Exploring the Amalfi Coast is not only for the elite; It is a paradise for all! Language barriers will not hinder your experience; Amalfi welcomes all with open arms! Planning a trip is never too complicated; Our guide simplifies your journey! The Amalfi Coast is not just for honeymooners; It is a solo adventurer's dream, too! You have seen it in pictures, but there is so much to discover; Prepare to be amazed! Discover the Amalfi Coast's hidden coves and secluded beaches. Indulge in authentic Italian cuisine overlooking the azure Tyrrhenian Sea. Immerse yourself in the rich history of Amalfi's ancient architecture. Unearth local traditions at vibrant markets and festivals. Capture Insta-worthy moments in the picturesque villages of Positano and Ravello. Savor the flavors of homemade limoncello in the heart of lemon orchards. Navigate the local transportation options like a seasoned traveler. Our guide shows you budget-friendly options for an affordable Amalfi adventure. Dive into the unfamiliar – Amalfi offers a unique experience beyond the ordinary. Our guide streamlines the planning process, ensuring a stress-free journey. If you want to transform your travel dreams into Amalfi realities, scroll up and click the 'Add to Cart' button now! Your enchanting journey awaits.

Unified Hearts
"Unified Hearts: Proven Strategies for Cultivating Lasting Marital Harmony in Blended Families" delves deeply into the art and science of nurturing a successful blended family. This insightful book unpacks the complexity of merging families, offering a rich tapestry of strategies, from effective communication and conflict resolution to emotional support and financial management. It emphasizes the importance of empathy, patience, and unconditional love in overcoming challenges and celebrates the joy of creating a united, supportive family environment. With expert advice, engaging exercises, and heartwarming success stories, "Unified Hearts" is an indispensable resource for couples seeking to build a strong foundation for their blended family, ensuring every member feels valued, understood, and integrated into the family dynamic.

Sky-Bound Dreams: A Guide to Becoming a Flight Attendant

Are you dreaming of a career that lets you soar above the clouds and explore new horizons? "Sky Bound Dreams: A Guide to Becoming a Flight Attendant" by Wanderlust Wren is your ultimate guide to turning those dreams into reality!

Packed with enthusiastic language and captivating stories, this book is perfect for readers of all ages who are eager to embark on an exciting journey in the aviation industry. From the magic of flying machines to the timeless glamour of the profession, "Sky Bound Dreams" covers everything you need to know to kick start your career as a flight attendant.

Inside, you'll find:

The Allure of the Skies: Discover the enchantment of aviation, the thrill of flying, and the endless possibilities that come with a career in the skies.

Preparing for Takeoff: Get practical advice on the educational requirements, certifications, and personal skills needed to become a successful flight attendant.

Navigating the Application Process: Learn how to craft a standout resume, write a compelling cover letter, and ace your interview with confidence.

In-Flight Excellence: Explore the day-to-day duties of a flight attendant, including safety protocols, customer service, and handling crisis situations with poise.

Embracing the Skies: Career Growth: Unlock the secrets to advancing your career, from climbing the ranks to exploring specializations and maintaining a healthy work-life balance.

With real-life anecdotes, inspiring stories, and expert tips, "Sky Bound Dreams" is more than just a guide—it's your passport to a fulfilling and adventurous career. Whether you're just starting out or looking to elevate your journey, this book will equip you with the knowledge and motivation to soar to new heights.

So, fasten your seat belt and prepare for takeoff. Your journey to becoming a flight attendant starts here with "Sky Bound Dreams: A Guide to Becoming a Flight Attendant" by Wanderlust Wren. Ready to reach for the skies? Let's fly!

Laugh & Color The Skies: Airplane Joke & Coloring Book

Ahoy, little captains and future aviators! Welcome aboard to "Laugh & Color the Skies: Airplane Joke & Coloring Book," where the sky's the limit, and your imagination flies!

Are you ready to embark on an epic coloring adventure? Climb aboard and explore the friendly skies with this fantastic coloring book filled with all sorts of airplanes, from speedy jets to mighty propellers! Get your crayons ready to add a splash of color to these magnificent flying machines!

Inside, you'll discover:

Exciting airplane designs just waiting for your creative touch! Color and enjoy some airplane jokes!

Plenty of room for you to unleash your creativity and make each airplane soar with your unique style!

So, buckle up and prepare for takeoff! Whether flying high or cruising low, "Laugh & Color the Skies: Airplane Joke & Coloring Book" promises hours of colorful fun and adventure for kids of all ages. Let's spread our wings and paint the skies with joy! Get ready to color, create, laugh and explore the amazing world of aviation like never before!

Printed in Great Britain
by Amazon